£11·99

WO
A Ed

ON

The 1970s and 1980s have seen an explosion of publishing by, about and for women. This new list is designed to make a particular contribution to this process by commissioning and publishing books which consolidate and advance feminist research and debate in key areas in a form suitable for students, academics and researchers but also accessible to a broader general readership.

As far as possible books will adopt an international perspective incorporating compara͙͙ ͙͙aterial from a range of countries where this is illumina͙ ͙͙ ͙͙ ͙͙ they will be interdisciplinary, aiming to put w͙ ͙͙ ͙͙inist discussion firmly on the agenda ir ͙͙ ͙͙ ͙͙ law, physical education, art an

A list of published and forthcoming ͙͙

In Her Own Write

Twentieth-Century Women's Fiction

Jennifer Breen

MACMILLAN

First published 1990

Published by
MACMILLAN EDUCATION LTD
Houndmills, Basingstoke, Hampshire RG21 2XS
and London
Companies and representatives
throughout the world

Photoset in Times by
Vine & Gorfin Ltd, Exmouth, Devon

Printed in Hong Kong

British Library Cataloguing in Publication Data
Breen, Jennifer
In Her Own Write: Twentieth-century
women's fiction.
1. Women's fiction in English, 1900—.Critical
studies
I. Title
823'.91'099287
ISBN 0–333–44791–3 (hardcover)
ISBN 0–333–44792–1 (paperback)

Series Standing Order

If you would like to receive future titles in this series as they are published,
you can make use of our standing order facility. To place a standing order
please contact your bookseller or, in case of difficulty, write to us at the
address below with your name and address and the name of the series. Please
state with which title you wish to begin your standing order. (If you live outside
the UK we may not have the rights for your area, in which case we will forward your
order to the publisher concerned.)

Standing Order Service, Macmillan Distribution Ltd,
Houndmills, Basingstoke, Hampshire, RG21 2XS, England.

To Mary (10), Katherine (8) and Roberta (6)

Contents

Acknowledgements

I am grateful to Jo Campling and Steve Kennedy for their editorial help, and to R. W. Noble for literary advice. Acknowledgements are also due to the Faculty of Humanities at the Polytechnic of North London for awarding me three months' leave so that I could begin to write this book.

JENNIFER BREEN

Introduction

Are the world-views in novels which have been written by women in the twentieth century much different from the world-views in fiction written by men? By 'world-view', I am referring, not to 'ideology', but to the whole conglomerate of ideas and beliefs, presumptions and assumptions, stereotypes and prejudices, and dreams and images which are embodied in each work of fiction for the amusement or boredom, emancipation or enslavement, and provocation or comfort of the reader.

In order to determine whether world-views in a work of fiction are conformist or seditious, we have to look at conflicts within each work and try to establish the point of view of the narrator. In Virginia Woolf's *Mrs Dalloway* (1925), for example, the narrator constructs in Clarissa Dalloway an upper middle-class woman who produces nothing spiritual or material except one child. This child, Elizabeth, is awakened, however, to the possibility of a professional career through which she would be able to take an equal place in the world with men. Miss Kilman, Elizabeth's governess, is mocked as a stereotypical feminist whose personal unattractiveness is exceeded only by her lesbian proclivities, which the narrator implicitly criticises, but elsewhere approves of in the relationship between Clarissa Dalloway and Sally Seton. The worlds of these characters metaphorically collide. Which one wins out in the narration of this novel? Evidently not Miss Kilman, since she is represented as a misguided feminist; and not Elizabeth, who in the end accepts her social position as a passive beauty. Marriage, with or without children, appears to be the most desirable goal for women, regardless of the personal cost of loss of freedom.

To conclude that *Mrs Dalloway* is a subversive text, therefore, would need special pleading in relation to its modernist form. On the other hand, Dorothy Richardson's *Pilgrimage*, vol. I (1915–17), can only be read as a mockery of 'patriarchy'. By 'patriarchy', I mean a society in which men are dominant in all the positions of power – police, military, industry, government, banking, civil service, trade unions, higher education and so on.[1] The exceptions like the Mrs Thatchers merely confirm the usual rule: men are dominant in most fields of public endeavour. By 'subversive', I mean any writing that shows up the *status quo* instead of supporting it. In the case of women writers, 'subversive' fiction is usually that which consciously or unconsciously undermines the received idea that men are superior to women and that men should dominate women. In the case of *Pilgrimage*, Richardson's narrator constructs and makes us want to identify with a heroine who consistently questions such a received view of why men should rule.

Even today, women who want the pleasures of heterosexual congress and motherhood usually end up being dominated by men. Such opting in merely confirms the fact that outdated assumptions about male and female social and economic roles are difficult to change. And although women are beginning to feel freer to write about their physical and emotional experiences as females, are we very often much further on from seeing ourselves as part of a man-made machine?

In much twentieth-century fiction, female characters are shown as doing more things, but mainly in bed. Women's fictional relationships often remain only sexual, and specifically between men and women; for instance, in D. H. Lawrence's *Women in Love* (1920) the conclusion embodies Rupert Birkin's defence of his need to have a close companionship with another man as well as to maintain his sexual relationship with Ursula, whereas Ursula must be satisfied with only a sexual relationship with Rupert. Women's relationships in actual life are multifarious – with employers, colleagues, neighbours, children, family members and so on – whereas in fiction such as D. H. Lawrence's novels, women's relationships are usually narrowed down to putative or actual sexual relationships with men. The way in which sexual relationships between men and women dominate the subject-matter of many of the most ambitious and acclaimed novels suggests that in twentieth-century society such relationships are more significant than any others. But this dominant world-view is beginning to be exposed in subversive fiction, especially by women.

In recent theories about the reading of literature, emphasis is laid not on the 'correct' reading of a text from the words on the page, but on looking at the way reading is related significantly to the reader's gender as well as to less significant factors such as class, education or nationality. Up to about 1970, literary criticism, like many other fields of intellectual endeavour, had been dominated by men, so that serious women readers in the past were encumbered with a mainly man-made guidance system. As early as 1929, Virginia Woolf distinguished for a large readership the man-made problems with which women novelists have had to cope:

> It is probable, however, that both in life and in art the values of a woman are not the values of a man. Thus, when a woman comes to write a novel, she will find that she is perpetually wishing to alter the established values – to make serious what appears insignificant to a man, and trivial what is to him important. And for that, of course, she will be criticized; for the critic of the opposite sex will be genuinely puzzled and surprised by an attempt to alter the current scale of values, and will see in it not merely a difference of view, but a view that is weak, or trivial, or sentimental, because it differs from his own.[2]

Woolf here specifies how women had begun to think about altering 'the current scale of values'. She also shows how male criticism of women's writing is impeded by male egotism. Women, according to Woolf, 'are coming to be more independent of opinion. They are beginning to respect their own sense of values'.

Woolf in 1929 also noted the beginning of some of the major changes that have occurred during the latter part of this century in some fiction by women:

> the subject matter of their novels begins to show certain changes. They are less interested, it would seem, in themselves; on the other hand, they are more interested in other women . . . women are beginning to explore their own sex, to write of women as women have never been written of before; for of course, until very lately, women in literature were the creation of men.
>
> Here again there are difficulties to overcome . . . Often nothing tangible remains of a woman's day. The food that has been cooked is eaten; the children that have been nursed have gone out into the world. Where does the accent fall? What is the salient point for the novelist to seize upon? It is difficult to say. Her life has an anonymous character which is baffling and puzzling in the extreme. For the first time, this dark country is beginning to be explored in fiction . . .[3]

But such fiction by women about other women as well as about the 'dark country' in women's experience tends to be either ignored or mocked in male-dominated literary journals and other publications.

And major changes did not occur in women's writing of criticism until the 1970s when a spate of women critics began to survey exactly what women had done in the arts as well as to show the gaps and falsifications in men's writing about women. Elaine Showalter, in *A Literature of Their Own: British Women Novelists from Brontë to Lessing* (1977), for example, traces a continuous tradition in women's fiction, although she does not attempt to distinguish closely between those works which subvert the *status quo* of male dominance and those which accept or even glorify the way things are for women in a patriarchal society. Moreover, she includes few original radical novelists of the 1960s and 1970s.[4] Patricia Stubbs, in *Women and Fiction: Feminism and the Novel 1880–1920* (1979), deconstructs some of the falsifications of women's sexuality which prevail in novels by early twentieth-century male authors such as H. G. Wells and Arnold Bennett, but she does not include in her study neglected but interesting women writers from the early twentieth century.[5]

One of my aims is to discover subversive meanings in underrated women's novels by reading this fiction in the light of theories about patriarchy, the unconscious, and gaps and silences in texts. Much of our contemporary interest in what has previously been repressed about women in both men's and women's fiction owes its origins to twentieth-century psychoanalytic theories about a postulated 'unconscious' which some feminists have taken up and applied to women to whom they refer metaphorically as the repressed 'Other'.[6] This metaphor of the repressed 'Other', whether it is used to refer to women or to any repressed social group, has become part of late twentieth-century dogma. I intend to assess the usefulness of applying this theory of the repressed 'Other' to the study of women's fiction in relation to the social world.

Nevertheless, I am not ditching the old tried and trousered methods of literary criticism such as analysing characterisation, discussing central themes in relation to plot, and assessing the aesthetic qualities of each work. But I shall stress how rewarding and instructive it is also to read using a scale of values that are favourable to women's multiple aspirations.

In order to explore the nature of twentieth-century women's writing, I have analysed texts which are original and subversive in their choice of subject. Thus I have included authors who write about physical and emotional experiences from a woman's point of view, who write about women at work, and who write about women engaged in subversive conflict with men.

But this guide is not an exhaustive survey of women's twentieth-century fiction, since the works of fiction I have chosen serve to illustrate my method of reading. Within any work of fiction, the skilled reader can discern a central voice – not necessarily that of the narrator, nor even the actual author – which reflects a construction of the distinctive point of view of the world in that work of fiction. The reader can then 'deconstruct' the given fiction by identifying gaps, contradictions and blind spots[7] as well as novelty, revelation and seditious departures in the world-view of each work.

1

The 'feminine' and fiction

What is a 'feminine' novel? By 'feminine', I mean not the more trivial constructions of what is considered 'feminine' in such areas of popular culture as make-up, perfumery, or soft porn videos, but those usually underrated qualities which convention now adduces to women: receptivity, diffuseness of emotionality, and intuitive thinking. Yet these conventions are by no means universal: Anthony Burgess finds 'clarity and common sense as essentially feminine properties in the novel' and cites Storm Jameson, Lettice Cooper, Vita Sackville-West and Nancy Mitford as illustrations of this definition of the 'feminine'. These women writers, he avers, 'have made our sweating male experimentalists look gauche and uncomfortable'. Burgess, as well as being selective in his reading of women's fiction, confuses 'feminine' with qualities that he projects into women.[1]

But feminists themselves give very different definitions of the 'feminine'. Hélène Cixous considers that a 'feminine' text is one that reveals the 'unconscious' or the repressed 'Other'. Cixous's metaphor of the repressed 'Other' has its origins in Freud's, Jung's and Lacan's psychoanalytic theories about the individual or collective 'unconscious' that supposedly lies repressed in us. All we can know about the 'unconscious' is acquired through dreams, slips of the pen or tongue, and free association, that is, saying or writing whatever comes into our minds without censorship.[2] Cixous postulates that the basis of the 'feminine' is the allowing of such a repressed 'Other' to break through into consciousness:

1

A feminine text cannot not be more than subversive: if it writes itself it is in volcanic heaving of the old 'real' property crust. In ceaseless displacement. She must write herself because, when the time comes for her liberation, it is the invention of a *new, insurgent* writing that will allow her to put the breaks and indispensable changes into effect in her history . . . Write yourself: your body must make itself heard. Then the huge resources of the unconscious will burst out.[3]

But allowing 'the unconscious' to 'burst out' in the manner that Cixous suggests is more likely to produce the raw material for art, rather than art itself. Art can never be the kind of 'feminine' therapy which Cixous seems to be proposing, although some of her subtler meaning might have been lost in the translation.

Cixous's notion of the 'unconscious' as a resource for writers, whether male or female, is not new. Wordsworth, in 'Intimations of Immortality from Recollections of Early Childhood' (1807) describes

> those first affections,
> Those shadowy recollections,
> Which, be they what they may,
> Are yet the fountain-light of all our day,
> Are yet a master-light of all our seeing . . .[4]

Wordsworth's phrase, 'shadowy recollections', refers to repressed or suppressed memories of childhood. And Keats's concept of 'Negative Capability' in the writer, which he describes as 'when man is capable of being in uncertainties, Mysteries, doubts, without any irritable reaching out after fact & reason',[5] reflects much of what Cixous describes as 'Other'. But Cixous appropriates this kind of Wordsworth–Keats Romantic incursion into the fluidity of the psyche as 'feminine': 'Rare are the men able to venture onto the brink where writing, freed from law, unencumbered by moderation, exceeds phallic authority, and where the subjectivity inscribing its effects becomes feminine.'[6] The subversion of patriarchy by means of subjectively asserting the writer's non-conformist individuality is, according to Cixous, a way of expressing what is 'feminine'.

But expression of the 'feminine' involves more than an overturning of patriarchal authority, and only a few male authors – and then only in some of their writing – have been able to overcome their addiction to authoritarianism and dominance, in order to imagine women's lives and aspirations in a way that is not merely male wish-fulfilment. A few, such as Patrick White and Joyce Cary, consistently construct women's characters who rise above men's stereotypes about women's behaviour, but even such unlikely masculine authors as Joseph Conrad and James Joyce have given us convincing women characters such as Winnie Verloc in *The Secret Agent* (1907) and Molly Bloom in *Ulysses* (1922). These two authors show imaginative flexibility in expressing areas of women's neglected or suppressed lives, even if their achievement has to be placed in the context of ignorance in Conrad's case and misogyny in Joyce's.

Though, as Hélène Cixous claims,[7] male authors such as James Joyce and Jean Genet are reasserting maternal and diffuse feminine sexual *jouissance* – both pre-verbal infantile and adult sexual pleasure – the world-view underlying much male fiction is that women can only be seen as an adjunct to men. Even James Joyce's invention of Molly Bloom, a character for whom he created a convincing voice which crackles with *aperçus* about women is based partly on a stock male fantasy about a type of woman whom many men might imagine themselves as measuring up to: the sexy woman thoughtlessly going after and pleasuring herself with virile men. Although many of us might admit to much the same fantasies as Joyce projects in Molly Bloom, there are not nearly enough Blazes Boylans to go round. Joyce makes us believe that Molly's 'stream of consciousness' recreates a woman's sexual fantasies, and he subverts the conventions and forms of the nineteenth-century novel with its logically ordered language. So far, so good. But elsewhere his fiction is nevertheless imbued with ideas about patriarchy being necessarily ascendant.

And why is it that women have taken a century longer than men to theorise the 'unconscious' as a source of material for art? Virginia Woolf was possibly the first to identify the problems a woman writer might have in expressing repressed areas of her mind:

> a novelist's chief desire is to be as unconscious as possible . . . I want you to imagine me writing a novel in a state of trance. I want you to figure for yourselves a girl sitting with a pen in her hand, which for minutes, and indeed for hours, she never dips into the inkpot . . . She was letting her imagination sweep unchecked round every rock and cranny of the world that lies submerged in the depths of our unconscious being . . . And then

there was a smash . . . she had thought of something, something about the body, about the passions which it was unfitting for her as a woman to say. Men, her reason told her, would be shocked. The consciousness of what men will say of a woman who speaks the truth about her passions had roused her from her artist's state of unconsciousness.[8]

Woolf is perhaps trying to explain her inability to write freely about her own sexuality in contrast with Joyce's appropriation of the freedom to express men and women's sexual fantasies in *Ulysses*. She adds that 'telling the truth about my own experiences as a body, I do not think I solved. I doubt that any woman has solved it yet.' The delay in the lowering of this barrier against women writers expressing themselves freely on sexual matters cannot merely be attributed to psychosexual hang-ups in women authors, since, if we are to judge by early twentieth-century women's fiction, this problem was widespread. In her 12-volume *Pilgrimage* (1915–38), Dorothy Richardson, despite her avant-garde form, also veers away from many possibilities of directly representing sexual fantasies.

Even in the late twentieth century, despite our supposed freedom to write about almost anything, Frankie Finn makes a statement which is comparable to Woolf's in that she also blames men for the imprisoning of women through false socialisation:

A phenomenon which most, probably all, women writers are aware of and in one way or another respond to, is the voice of male censure, both inside and outside. It is the censure which has shaped our lives, the male audience we have been taught to please, the authoritative weight of literature, the lover who applauds our gestures as victim.[9]

Despite the desire of some women authors to write about their 'feminine' feelings, potentialities and values, they have been, and continue to be impeded by the fear of what men will say about such writing. Both Woolf and Finn seem to define the 'feminine' in terms of their sexuality, suggesting that male influence prevents them writing about what is for them 'feminine'. Only when women have remade their own view of themselves and internalised a new scale of values will they be free of that masculine super-ego which, through sociocultural training, they have more or less imposed on themselves.

So what is 'feminine' writing? Or do all good writers of fiction have to embrace a kind of androgyny? Most of us have both male and female components in our psyches. Patrick White, in his comment on differences in male and female behaviour in Australia, reminds us that men can be feminine and women masculine:

> the little that is subtle in the Australian character comes from the masculine principle in its women, the feminine in its men. Alas, the feminine element in the men is not strong enough to make them more interesting.[10]

Feminists seem to be hung up on the notion of asserting their difference from, even superiority to men. Much might be gained by marrying the exceptional qualities of masculinity with those of femininity, at least in the sphere of writing. Most of all, women need to assert, not their difference, but their equal status in society with men.

Among 'modernist' writers, Dorothy Richardson is probably the first to have subverted the *status quo* of unequal relations between men and women *as well as* to have subverted the conventions of novel writing as a form. Literary historians find in Richardson a successor to Henry James, who had already written novels such as *The Ambassadors* (1903) from the point of view or consciousness of one character. But Richardson took this method a stage further by inventing the 'stream of consciousness' which shows in detail how the mind of a young woman relates to the external world without her thoughts seeming to be mediated by a narrator. Richardson, unlike the later Joyce, does not use interior monologue as part of her heroine's stream of consciousness, but employs free indirect discourse throughout *Pilgrimage*: that is, a covert narrator presents in the third person what Miriam Henderson is thinking and at times gives the reader first-person phrases of Miriam. This method of narration creates the illusion that Miriam is in the throes of conceptualising these thoughts, as well as allowing the narrator to comment implicitly on those thoughts.

The following passage, for example, in which Miriam ruminates over her abilities as a teacher of English in a German boarding-school for girls, is contrived to suggest Miriam's interior thoughts as well as to convey part of the narrative to the reader:

> It was a fool's errand . . . To undertake to go to the German school and teach . . . to be going there . . . with nothing to give. The moment would come when there would be a class sitting round a table waiting for her to speak. She imagined one of the rooms at the old school, full of scornful

girls . . . How was English taught? How did you begin? English grammar . . . in German? Her heart beat in her throat. She had never thought of that . . . the rules of English grammar? Parsing and analysis . . . Anglo-Saxon prefixes and suffixes . . . gerundial infinitive . . . It was too late to look anything up. Perhaps there would be a class tomorrow . . . The German lessons at school had been dreadfully good . . . Fraulein's grave face . . . her perfect knowledge of every rule . . . her clear explanations in English . . . her examples . . . All these things were there, in English grammar . . . And she had undertaken to teach them and could not even speak German.[11]

Here the impersonal narrator describes broken phrases, such as 'Fraulein's grave face' from Miriam's supposed consciousness. Miriam's anxiety about teaching English language to German adolescent girls brings back fragmented memories of the way in ·which she was taught German at her own school.

One of the problems for the author of this kind of narration is how to suggest the minutiae of everyday experience without giving the reader every minute of her character's day. At times Richardson adds commonplace details which might assist verisimilitude, but which some readers, especially male ones, describe as dull. Yet for female readers who, like Miriam, often find themselves in positions in which they are dominated by, or at least subordinate to men, the whole of *Pilgrimage*, highs and lows, is exhilarating, since the fictional Miriam spends much of her time finding out about herself in relation to men. *Pilgrimage* is punctuated with Miriam's moments of insight about the actual state of things in contrast with her fantasies.

Richardson, according to her contemporary, Virginia Woolf, has invented a language which is suitable for the 'feminine gender'. Here Woolf is using the word 'feminine' to mean writing which is intrinsic to women authors only:

She has invented, or, if she has not invented, developed and applied to her own uses, a sentence which we might call the psychological sentence of the feminine gender. It is of a more elastic fibre than the old, capable of stretching to the extreme, of suspending the frailest particles, of enveloping the vaguest shapes. Other writers of the opposite sex have used sentences of this description and stretched them to the extreme. But there is a difference. Miss Richardson has fashioned her sentence consciously, in order that it may descend to the depths and investigate the crannies of Miriam Henderson's consciousness. It is a woman's sentence, but only in the sense that it is used to describe a woman's mind by a writer who is neither proud nor afraid of anything that she may discover in the psychology of her sex.[12]

Woolf suggests that Richardson's writing is different from that of an intuitive male author since she is the first to explore in fiction the depths of a woman's mind. But, surprisingly, Woolf does not see fit to comment on the fact that in *Pilgrimage* Richardson eschews description of her heroine's 'experiences as a body', even if she could be said to speak the truth about Miriam Henderson's 'passions'.

The obvious technical difference in the style of *Pilgrimage* is the use of elisions to suggest fragmentary thought processes in the consciousness of the main character, Miriam. Richardson's method of representing disconnected thought processes has not been much imitated. Thus, particularly in her use of syntax, Richardson has at times broken up the then conventional form of sentence construction in novels, expressing a 'feminine' content in a 'feminine' style. But this style is also a possibility for men, since the male author, Joyce Cary, later achieved a similar effect in his characterisation of Nina in *A Prisoner of Grace* (1952).

As Woolf remarks, Richardson's style amounts to more than innovations in form. In the development of Miriam's consciousness – which can be seen entirely as a representation of the 'dark country' of neglected aspects of women's imaginings – the narrative thrust exposes her gradual understanding of her lot as a woman in relation to the patriarchal order in that world. In the following episode, for example, Miriam is shown reacting critically to male sermons in a way which ridicules the pretensions of male preachers:

> . . . you could not stop a sermon. It was so unfair. The services might be lovely, if you did not listen to the words; and then the man got up and went on and on from unsound premises until your brain was sick . . . droning on and on, and getting more and more pleased with himself and emphatic . . . and nothing behind it. As often as not you could pick out the logical fallacy if you took the trouble . . . Preachers knew no more than anyone else. . .[13]

Religion for Miriam is imposed by the patriarchal order under which she lives. The narrator, by jumping from one thought to another as if Miriam were irrational, actually subverts the masculine so-called wisdom that thought needs to be ordered.

Most criticism of fiction up to the late 1970s has been from the point of view of the middle-class male, and fictional experiences such as Miriam's apparently frivolous but actually serious realisation of the patriarchal distortion of religious practices have been discounted. Yet the fictionalised Miriam's relationship to patriarchy is just as important and interesting as Stephen Dedalus's fictionalised relationship with his mother, Mother Church and mother country in *Portrait of the Artist as a Young Man* (1916). Joyce's novel is thought to be concerned with something important – how Stephen freed himself from the 'maternal' death-hug. Yet Joyce's narrator's ascription of the source of constraint to mothering is a form of scapegoating as well as a 'fiction'. The world-views of both *Portrait of the Artist as a Young Man* and *Ulysses* can be seen as being oriented towards the rejection of women, mainly through Joyce's symbolic representations of the maternal as the enslaving or smothering force in his hero's life. The historical fact is that the Stephens of Ireland were constricted by a bunch of male clerics and nationalist patriarchs – the type of patriarch that Richardson's heroine, Miriam, criticises.

Katherine Mansfield, like Richardson, is a 'feminine' writer in that she deals in an appropriate style with what has been neglected or distorted about women. In 1915, she tried out an impressionistic style in *The Aloe* (which she revised and published in 1918 as *Prelude*). In conveying the inner world of Linda, her heroine, in *The Aloe*, she consistently punctuates her thoughts with dashes, which has the effect of suggesting an impulsive bursting-forth of suppressed feeling in Linda:

If only he didn't jump up at her and bark so loudly and thump with his tail and watch her with such eager loving eyes! He was too strong for her. She always *had* hated things that rushed at her even when she was a child – There were times when he was frightening – really frightening, when she just hadn't screamed at the top of her voice – 'you are killing me' – and when she had longed to say the most coarse hateful things . . . for all her love and respect and admiration she hated him. It had never been so plain to her as it was at this moment – There were all her 'feelings' about Stanley one just as true as the other – sharp defined – She could have done them up in little packets – and there was this other – just as separate as the rest, this hatred and yet just as real. She wished she had done them up in little packets and given them to Stanley – especially the last one – she would like to watch him while he opened that. . .[14]

This transmogrification, through Linda's satirical viewpoint, of her husband into a 'Newfoundland dog' is a humorous evocation of a woman's perceptions which subvert male dominance.

In Stanley's own inner life, the narrator plays on a malaise which is common in the twentieth-century male – a half-hidden anxiety underlying patriarchal self-satisfaction:

> A sort of panic overtook Burnell whenever he approached near home. Before he was well inside the gate he would shout to anyone in sight, 'is everything all right?' and then he did not believe it was until he heard Linda cry 'Hello, you old boy!'[15]

But the reader knows that his unease in his dominating role is not without some foundation. Linda mocks both marriage and husband openly, and has secret fantasies about leaving him and her three daughters. The bleak comedy of Burnell's situation is intensified by the narrator's depiction of his complacent egotism:

> It was a familiar cry in the house 'Linda's wedding ring has *gone again* – Stanley Burnell could never hear that without a horrible sense of discomfort. Good Lord! he wasn't superstitious – He left that kind of rot to people who had nothing better to think about – but all the same, it was *devilishly* annoying. Especially as Linda made so light of the affair and mocked him and said 'are they as expensive as all that' and laughed at him and cried, holding up her bare hand – 'Look, Stanley, it has all been a dream'. He was a fool to mind things like that, but they hurt like sin.[16]

The lord and master must not be mocked, nor must the sign of his dominance be ridiculed.

Behind Stanley's back, Linda is even more cruelly mocking; for example, she jokes about the new house and land that Stanley has just bought for them, suggesting that it will 'be flooded from the autumn to the spring' and that 'Stanley will have to row to the office in an open boat. He'd love that. I can imagine the glow he would arrive in and the way he'd measure his chest twice a day to see how fast it was expanding.'[17] Mansfield's earlier caricature of Burnell's get-fit exercises in which Linda reassures him – "'Yes my dear don't worry you'll never be fat – You're far too energetic"'[18] – shows us that, although Linda might seem to acquiesce in wifely submission in her relations with her husband, she is actually humorously parodying the role she is supposed to be performing. As she tells her mother when she refuses to look over the house Stanley has bought for them, "'I'll satisfy Stanley. Besides I can *rave* all the better over what I haven't seen."'[19] The narrator reveals the underside of Linda's prosperous marriage, exposing her dissatisfaction which she politically never expresses overtly to Stanley. He is forced to pretend that he does not notice her hurtful remarks.

Burnell has built his emotional security on the shaky foundations of patriarchal dominance of the supposedly capricious and unfathomable female. But Linda is not shown to the reader as capricious, although she might seem so to her husband. Her behaviour is a self-serving response to her imprisonment in her marriage, which to her is an outrage. Her feeling of imprisonment stems mainly from her economic dependence on Stanley, so much so that she is afraid to express openly her enjoyment in being with women. Her mother, Mrs Fairfield, takes on the role of society's agent of oppression since she tries to coerce Linda into behaving as docilely in her marriage as she believed women were supposed to do. Mrs Fairfield epitomises the kind of older woman who thinks it her duty to induct younger women into their supposedly ordained role of subservience to men.

In *The Aloe*, Mansfield brings out into the open the conventional suppression of women's inner feelings, especially in the institution of marriage, where women have traditionally been given a social, sexual and economic role to which they must conform if they wish to remain married. All the characters in *The Aloe*, apart from Mrs Fairfield, have vivid fantasies which reveal the underside of their superficially happy worlds. Beryl, Linda's unmarried sister, lives on dreams of finding an ideal lover, although, because she is economically dependent on her sister and brother-in-law, her existence seems fruitless; 'One may as well rot here as anywhere else',[20] she soliloquises about the Burnells' new house. Another sister who is married vents her frustration in vengeful dreams about her mother and Linda. Even the servant simmers with rebellion in her relations with one of her superiors, Beryl.

Perhaps the significance of the aloe tree is that it symbolises the unusualness of fulfilment in women, since only Linda's mother is shown as enjoying living fruitfully in her domestic surroundings. Linda tells her daughter, Kezia, that the aloe tree flowers only 'once every hundred years' and, later in the story, Mrs Fairfield suggests that the aloe '"is going to flower – this year. Wouldn't that be wonderfully lucky!" '[21] But Linda notices 'the long sharp thorns that edged the Aloe leaves, and at the sight of them her heart grew hard.' She imagines that the aloe tree is a ship that will carry her away from her sexual unease: 'She particularly liked the long sharp thorns. Nobody would dare to come near her ship or to follow after. "Not even my Newfoundland dog [Stanley]." '[22]

Throughout this novel, a sub-text reveals how women react in their imaginative lives when their direct responses to life are distorted or even repressed. In particular, the characterisation of Beryl is used in order to show how, in a patriarchal society, unmarried women are expected to respond receptively to any supposedly attractive male who attempts a flirtation. In fact, sexuality is portrayed as a satisfying possibility only for men. Children might result from such sexual engagements, and some women, such as Linda's mother, find satisfaction from their nurture. Linda, however, does not, but nevertheless sustains herself in her spiritual prison by implicitly mocking Stanley and secretly making up fantasies about leaving him.

Although the world of a novel is not an embodiment of the author's beliefs about her actual world, a fictional world often implies a world-view that can be deduced from the way the behaviour of the characters is constructed in that fictional world. Both Richardson and Mansfield have made up characters who attempt a deconstruction of the male authoritarian society in which they are placed, whereas Woolf and Joyce in their fiction on the whole create characters who accept the constraints of the patriarchal order, or what Lacan called 'the Law of the Father'.[23]

But Woolf, unlike Joyce, makes no attempt to narrate in the first person the actual thought processes of her characters. Instead, like Richardson and Mansfield, she employs free indirect discourse, that is, the use of a third-person narrator who incorporates some of the first-person speech of characters in order to reveal them. We might expect that Virginia Woolf, who dwelt on the unequal position of women *vis-à-vis* men extensively in her prose, but especially in *Three Guineas* (1938), would also in fiction expose that authoritarian male-dominated society. But Woolf's novels create fictional worlds which, on the whole, apart from occasional incidental irony at men's expense, tend to endorse the *status quo* of inequality for women in English society.

In *To the Lighthouse* (1927), for example, a conflict is displayed between support of patriarchal organisation and dissent from it. At Mrs Ramsay's dinner party, Lily Briscoe, the artist, sets out to undermine the stereotypical behaviour that is expected of women, but is shown as unable to defeat Mrs Ramsay's silent yet powerful intervention:

> There is a code of behaviour she knew, whose seventh article (it may be) says that on occasions of this sort it behoves the woman, whatever her own occupation may be, to go to the help of the young man opposite so that he may expose and relieve the thigh bones, the ribs, of his vanity, of his urgent desire to assert himself; as indeed it is their duty, she reflected, in her old maidenly fairness, to help us, suppose the Tube were to burst into flames. Then, she thought, I should certainly expect Mr Tansley to get me out. But how would it be, she thought, if neither of us did either of these things? So she sat there smiling . . . if Mrs Ramsay said to her as in effect she did, 'I am drowning, my dear, in seas of fire. Unless you apply some balm to the anguish of this hour and say something nice to that young man there, life will run upon the rocks – indeed I hear the grating and the growling at this minute. My nerves are taut as fiddle strings. Another touch and they will snap – when Mrs Ramsay said all this, as the glance in her eyes said it, of course for the hundred and fiftieth time Lily Briscoe had to renounce the experiment – what happens if one is not nice to that young man there – and be nice.[24]

Through Lily's eyes, the narrator ironically suggests the young man's 'vanity'. But, although Lily is shown as seeing through both Tansley's need to feed his ego with her admiration and Mrs Ramsay's desire to aggrandise her powers as a hostess, she is not able to undermine the weight of this social oppression. Moreover, the narrator presents the reader with no possibility of change in the *status quo* of relations between men and women:

> [Lily] had done the usual trick – been nice. She would never know him. He would never know her. Human relations were all like that, she thought, and the worst . . . were between men and women. Inevitably these were extremely insincere.[25]

Although the narrator takes an ironic stance throughout this novel to the way in which women continually support the damaged egos of men, Mrs Ramsay is on the whole still presented as an ideally socialised woman, and Lily bows to her silent request that social conventions be met. The gap or blind spot in *To the Lighthouse* is the unacknowledged conflict between adherence to the values of a

patriarchal system – which are as destructive to men as to women –
and denunciation of them. The form of *To the Lighthouse*, with its
ellipses and narrational jumps from one consciousness to another,
subverts the order of a conventionally well-made novel and implies
some mockery of prevailing philosophies about the need for
rationality in any form of discourse. Yet the world-view of this work
tends to endorse the way things are for women in a patriarchy.

In her treatment of characters set in the lower classes, the
narrator reflects the world-view of that period that servants were
necessarily unable to think or to meditate. The portrait of Mrs
McNab in *To the Lighthouse*, for example, shows her to be, in the
eyes of the narrator, an inevitable part of society and not one of its
female victims:

> As she lurched (for she rolled like a ship at sea) and leered (for her eyes
> fell on nothing directly, but with a sidelong glance that deprecated the
> scorn and anger of the world – she was witless, she knew it), as she
> clutched the banisters and hauled herself upstairs and rolled from room
> to room, she sang.[26]

To try to reconstruct imaginatively the soul of a cleaner is
innovatory, but this recreation is from a patronising point of view
which is emphasised by phrases such as 'she was witless, she knew
it'. If Mrs McNab were witless, she would not be likely to realise her
lack. The implied author who can be reconstructed from a reading
of *To the Lighthouse* seems essentially of white middle-class
extraction. Moreover, she does not wish to quarrel with her implied
reader about society's attitude to gender or class.

Although in this novel two types of women are portrayed – the
maternal Mrs Ramsay and the artistic Lily Briscoe – these two
possibilities for women are seen as separate and distinct. Lily, the
artist, remains a spinster, while Mrs Ramsay, who dies suddenly in
the middle of her career as a mother, lives on only through her
family. This dichotomy between artist and mother persists
throughout the novel, as in the following passage, where Mrs
Ramsay advises Lily:

> . . . they all must marry, since in the whole world, whatever laurels might
> be tossed to her (but Mrs Ramsay cared not a fig for her painting), or
> triumphs won by her (probably Mrs Ramsay had had her share of those),
> and here she saddened, darkened, and came back to her chair, there

could be no disputing this: an unmarried woman (she lightly took [Lily's] hand for a moment), an unmarried woman has missed the best of life. The house seemed full of children sleeping and Mrs Ramsay listening; of shaded lights and regular breathing.[27]

Mrs Ramsay, however, is neither the voice of the narrator, nor of Virginia Woolf, but is a fictional construct. And the crux of this novel lies in the artist finding that the maternal is a source of inspiration outside herself. Lily finds a way to the completion of her picture in a vision she has of the now dead Mrs Ramsay:

Mrs Ramsay – it was part of her perfect goodness to Lily – sat there quite simply, in the chair, flicked her needles to and fro, knitted her reddish-brown stocking, cast her shadow on the step . . . There it was – her picture. Yes, with all its green and blues, its lines running up and across, its attempt at something. It would be hung in the attics, she thought; it would be destroyed. But what did that matter? she asked herself, taking up her brush again. She looked at the steps; they were empty; she looked at her canvas; it was blurred. With a sudden intensity, as if she saw it clear for a second, she drew a line there, in the centre. It was done; it was finished. Yes, she thought, laying down her brush in extreme fatigue, I have had my vision.[28]

The artist triumphs here over the mother, since the maternal is merely the object of the artist's imagination in the same way that the female Muse is seen as a source of inspiration for men.

Is Woolf 'feminine' or 'feminist'? To be 'feminine' – to realise one's powers of intuitive imagining and to reveal in characters such as Mrs Dalloway and Mrs Ramsay the quintessential Blooms-buryian perfecting of the refined sensibility – is not sufficient to bring about change in relationships between men and women. The Mrs Dalloways of our world could be cast fictionally as MPs with party-giving husbands, and the Mrs Ramsays could be shown taking degrees in philosophy and writing books in the time provided by their husbands who have agreed to share child care. Some twentieth-century fiction by women portrays worlds in which women do more then establish personal relationships and, if they embrace the work of the artist, they also engage in a sexual life as male artists have always done.

To a limited extent then, *To the Lighthouse* might be read as a partial critique of a society under a patriarchal government, since Mr Ramsay, in his egocentricity and narcissism, is represented as

morally inferior to his ever-serving, unselfish wife. When Mr
Ramsay behaves like an autocratic monster, Mrs Ramsay expends
her energy in trying to soothe him. But, because their marriage
reflects the ideal held up by society for heterosexual marriage, it is
difficult to read this novel as a critique in fiction of that ideal. The
sole subversion of the ideals of patriarchy occurs in Lily Briscoe's
dismissal of Charles Tansley's comment, '[Women] can't paint;
[women] can't write'.[29]

What is more noticeable in *To the Lighthouse* than this split
between women's careers as artist and/or mother, is the split
between women's physical and mental experiences. Both Mrs
Ramsay's and Lily Briscoe's experiences are on a metaphysical
plane. At Mrs Ramsay's dinner party, the food is symbolic rather
than tangible, and Lily's painting is about 'vision' rather than the
textures of the materials with which she is working. As Woolf
herself complained, like other women writers of fiction she never
got to grips with women's physical existence in the way that James
Joyce did, particularly in *Ulysses*. Even Mrs Ramsay's departure
from corporeality is quickly passed over.

Nor is Dorothy Richardson's Miriam, although she is liberated
enough at that period to work for her living as teacher and dentist's
assistant, shown as referring to the whole area of women's bodily
functions, such as menstruation or orgasm. Yet *Pilgrimage* does
present in Miriam Henderson a character who consistently
questions the received social order of her period. In the following
excerpt, for example, she questions the value of marriage for herself
with its consequent loss of freedom:

> Why did men always have more freedom?. . .
> Adam had not faced the devil. He was stupid first, and afterwards a
> coward and a cad . . . 'the divine curiosity of Eve . . .' Some parson had
> said that . . . Perhaps men would turn round one day and see what they
> were like. Eve had not been unkind to the devil; only Adam and God.
> All the men in the world, and their God, ought to apologize to women.
> . . .
> To hold back and keep free . . . and real. Impossible to be real unless
> you were quite free. . . .
> But money.
> The chair-bed creaked as she knelt up and turned out the gas. 'I love
> you' . . . just a quiet manly voice . . . perhaps one would forget
> everything, all the horrors and mysteries . . . because there would be
> somewhere then always to be, to rest, and feel sure. If only . . . just to sit

hand in hand . . . watching snowflakes . . . to sit in the lamplight, quite quiet.[30]

Through the narrator, Miriam rewrites the Adam and Eve myth in order to present Eve in a more sympathetic light, implying that curiosity about sex is natural, and that men, through their myth about that archetypal man, Adam, have denied their feeling of curiosity and displaced it onto Eve.

In her relationship with her mother, which we invariably see from only Miriam's point of view, is epitomised the half-used life of women who marry and have children, but have no work of their own:

> 'My life has been so useless,' said Mrs Henderson suddenly.
> Here it was . . . a jolt . . . an awful physical shock, jarring her body . . . She braced herself and spoke quickly and blindly . . . a network of feeling vibrated all over to and fro, painfully.
> 'It only seems so to you,' she said, in a voice muffled by the beating of her heart. Anything might happen – she had no power . . . Mother – almost killed by things she could not control, having done her duty all her life . . . doing thing after thing had not satisfied her . . . being happy and brave had not satisfied her. There was something she had always wanted, for herself . . . even mother. . . .
> Mrs Henderson shuddered and sighed. Her pose relaxed a little.
> 'I might have done something for the poor.'[31]

This representation of Mrs Henderson as a dutiful mother who has always wanted more than motherhood underlines the split that existed at that period between a professional career and motherhood.

Richardson, despite her 'stream-of-consciousness' technique, is not as subversive of the form of the novel as is Joyce who in *Ulysses* (1922) regularly employs the first-person voice of his characters in the representation of their interior monologues, and in *Finnegan's Wake* (1939) restructures language itself. Nevertheless, Richardson is a trail-breaker in her creation of the internal world of an early twentieth-century woman seeking truths about the male–female balance of power. The world of *Pilgrimage* reveals a society in which patriarchal values dominate and in which marriage is pictured as the *sine qua non* of any young woman's aims in life, but Miriam becomes gradually disillusioned with these values. She finds freedom for herself in discovering her individuality. In her mind,

Miriam subverts the patriarchal world of the novel, which implies for any female reader that she might do the same in the world in which she finds herself.

Through their narrators, both Richardson and Mansfield expose their male-run worlds to a radical critique. But Woolf's narrator in, for example, *To the Lighthouse*, encourages the reader to think that the inequalities in women's lot *vis-à-vis* men are inevitable. Woolf reveals something of women's 'dark country', but is less revelatory than either Richardson or Mansfield. Both *Pilgrimage* and *The Aloe* in their respective ways enlighten us about women's roles in our past and current world. Unlike Woolf, who gives us a maternally sufficient Mrs Ramsay and a fulfilled artist in Lily Briscoe, Richardson and Mansfield present us with disgruntled twentieth-century women who are unhappy with life and unhappy with heterosexuality, whether these women characters are single or married, artistic or materialistic.

But in literary history, Richardson has been relegated to the position of a precursor to 'modernism', which, combined with the length of her 12-volume *Pilgrimage*, has militated against her work being read. Mansfield, who is just beginning to make a comeback, is nevertheless usually 'placed', at least in the mainstream press, as a descendant of Chekov, rather than as a 'feminine' subversive writer.

Differences between 'feminine' and 'masculine' are immaterial in a world in which the qualities of both are useful to the well-rounded personality. Men might realise that to adopt aspects of the 'feminine' – say, in child care or other relationships – is not a living death to their masculinity. Men might redefine the social construct, 'masculinity', to include 'feminine' attributes of care and nurture. Women might also find masculine drive and order of some use in, say, the business world. What women need most of all is not a boosting of their 'feminine' qualities but equal treatment in all spheres with men. And some twentieth-century fiction opens up these kinds of possibilities for both men and women.

2

Sexuality and marriage

In fiction by men this century, representations of heterosexual behaviour have often been nothing more than an increasingly detailed vulgarisation of entrenched beliefs and prejudices about women's sexual roles as servicer and victim of men. In *Sexual Politics*, Kate Millett's analyses of fiction by Henry Miller, Norman Mailer and D. H. Lawrence reveal in their work a consistent dehumanising of women in men's sexual behaviour towards them.[1] Their fiction could be said to act as a partial mirror of life which is tarnished by bias and prejudice. Gaps and blind spots, which feminists such as Millett have tried to expose, abound in their work. Yet, although women this century have become increasingly free to write openly in fiction about sexual relations, not many have used this possibility to advantage in order to reveal the inequality of women's sexual roles *vis-à-vis* those of men.

Most fiction by women about sexual lust and love can be divided conveniently, if crudely, into two categories: works which tend to endorse stereotyped roles for women as romantic lovers, wives or mothers, and those which, through the fictionalising of alternative possibilities, question such stereotyping. Rosamond Lehmann's *The Weather in the Streets* (1936) exemplifies fiction which supports the *status quo* of male–female relations. In this novel, the love-obsessed heroine, Olivia, accepts her position as a part-time mistress to a first-class male chauvinist, Rollo, who is already married. At the conclusion, Olivia submits unquestioningly to Rollo's illicit sexual domination of her:

> So stupid, to make a fuss [Olivia thinks]. A little rift, an unfortunate misunderstanding – over now. One must see things in proportion.

18

'I should so terribly miss our lunches', [Rollo] was saying with soft persistence.

So should I. They were so pleasant.

'Our drives. . .'

Oh, yes, the drives, they were so pleasant. Why not a lunch, a drive, if he wanted to, very discreetly, now and then? . . . It was all so pleasant. . .[2]

Nothing in this text indicates that we should read Olivia's unspoken thoughts as ironic, although we might wish to do so. And yet the 'little rift' had led to Olivia's painful abortion of her and Rollo's child. Olivia is not able to free herself from him in order to develop her own life, a situation which the narrator implicitly accepts.

Such romanticising about women's passive roles in relation to men has a long tradition in women's fiction, but the inability of women critics to question this tradition in the light of women's political emancipation is striking. A stream of such novels has been taken seriously by both female and male critics this century. Elizabeth Bowen's *The Last September* (1929), for example, gives the impression that a woman's only significance is in her capacity to 'love' sexually. Although the Irish 'troubles' of the 1920s impinge on the action of this novel, the central focus is on upper middle- or upper-class non-working females whose main purpose in life is apparently to amuse and to service, at dances and tennis parties, their British officer–lovers. Bowen's *The House in Paris* (1935) concentrates on the feelings of an illegitimate boy who longs for his natural mother as well as legitimacy. But again, through the intimations of the narrator, we are encouraged to think that 'love' – meaning an overwhelming sexual passion – is more important than fidelity to friends, especially women friends. By the conclusion of this novel, married affection, if not love, as shown in the relations between Karen and her husband, Ray Forestier, becomes the norm. Such a resolution is not surprising, given Karen's acceptance of her mother's 'view', which is set out early in the narrative, that 'a woman's real life only began with marriage, that girlhood amounts to no more than a privileged looking on'.[3] Since the narrator makes no ironic comment on this statement, the reader is left to suppose that this assertion expresses the implicit ideology of the novel.

Among other female novelists whose works centre on various permutations of unequal sexual relationships between men and women are the sisters, Margaret Drabble and A. S. Byatt.

Drabble's fiction up to and including *The Needle's Eye* (1973) is analysed by Elaine Showalter in *A Literature of Their Own: British Women Novelists from Brontë to Lessing* (1977; revised 1982). Showalter concludes that Drabble is forcing 'the ideology of marriage on a fiction straining to go beyond it . . . Drabble has been increasingly ambitious, serious, and open-minded; her work is the record of a feminine consciousness expanding and maturing'.[4] Yet in later novels, such as *The Middle Ground* (1980), Drabble, like other contemporary British novelists such as Anita Brookner and Penelope Lively, is still addicted to admiring, if not preserving, the *status quo* by producing novels about women's relationships with men, whether within marriage or out of it. *The Middle Ground* concludes with the sexually buccaneering Kate's rhapsodical dreams for herself: 'Will she herself abandon all hesitation and agree to fly out to Baghdad with Hugo, will she find a voice in which to speak, at last, to Ted, there, amongst so many people? Will she fall in love with Ruth's Rastaman?'[5] Or it could be Tom, Dick, or Harry – the message is the same: women's central purpose is to find a man, or even men, on whom to depend, whatever else they manage to do with their lives.

A. S. Byatt's fiction covers much the same ground as her sister's, that is, sex within marriage or outside it. But whereas Drabble merely nods politely in the direction of art (a reference to *Mrs Dalloway*, for example, in *The Middle Ground*), Byatt concentrates two of her novels, *The Virgin in the Garden* (1980) and *Still Life* (1985) on the relationship between art and life through her characterisation of the male dramatist, Alexander Wedderburn. Byatt nevertheless tries to reveal some of the contemporary dilemmas of women; for example, she shows that having children and a career is a problem for women but not for men.

Some women novelists outside the dominant tradition of fiction have produced writing which attempts to subvert the *status quo* of the received notion that all that women need in order to attain happiness is the sexual love of a man. And we do not have to wait for the so-called 'second-wave feminism' of the late 1960s and early 1970s to discover novelists who show us through their fictional worlds the fallacy of letting heterosexual love dominate our lives. Not only have these novelists questioned some of the received ideas about the institution of marriage, but they have also depicted its violence and disillusion, especially, but not always, for women.

These outsiders' subversion of accepted conventions about marriage can be seen at the turn of the century in Kate Chopin's *The Awakening* (1899) and Miles Franklin's *My Brilliant Career* (1901). In *The Awakening*, the central character, Edna Pontellier, finds herself imprisoned in a marriage which provides little sexual companionship or fulfilment. The demands of truth might suggest that when she finds herself aroused by a man two years younger than herself, Robert Lebrun, she should be freed from her unsatisfying marriage. But social conventions of that period about a woman's duty towards her husband and children bind Edna to Mr Pontellier. The latter's qualities as husband are characteristic of 'gentlemen' in the Deep South at the turn of the century. He reacts, for example, to her sunburn: '"You are burnt beyond recognition" he added, looking at his wife as one looks at a valuable piece of personal property which has suffered some damage.'[6] This treatment of Edna as an object that he possesses has a deleterious effect on her: 'An indescribable oppression, which seemed to generate in some unfamiliar part of her consciousness, filled her whole being with a vague anguish.'[7] Her marriage has come about by 'accident, in this respect resembling many other marriages which masquerade as the decrees of Fate'.[8] Edna in early womanhood had a penchant for becoming infatuated with certain faces of men, such as that of a great actor, and it was in the midst of 'her great passion' for this 'tragedian' that she succumbed to Leonce Pontellier's courtship: 'As the devoted wife of a man who worshipped her, she felt she would take her place with a certain dignity in the world of reality, closing the portals forever behind her upon the realm of romance and dreams.'[9] But she has made a mistake: the world of reality with a husband who does not sexually arouse her forces her back to the world of romance in the shape of Robert, who habitually falls in love with married women. When he tries to escape commitment to her, she makes do with Arrobus, a roué who stimulates her lust.

Moreover, Edna is not a 'mother woman' and does not like the work of managing her children: 'Their absence . . . seemed to free her of a responsibility which she had blindly assumed and for which Fate had not fitted her.'[10] She realises that she does not wish to sacrifice herself for them, preferring 'to do as she liked and feel as she liked'.[11] She consequently decides to live separately from her husband and children in order to explore her sexuality, but she realises that her love for men is a chimera:

Despondency had come upon her there in the wakeful night, and had never lifted. There was no one thing in the world that she desired. There was no human being whom she wanted near her except Robert; and she even realized that the day would come when he, too, and the thought of him would melt out of her existence, leaving her alone. The children appeared before her like antagonists who had overcome her, who had overpowered and sought to drag her into the soul's slavery for the rest of her days. But she knew a way to elude them.[12]

She drowns herself, not because she has penetrated the illusion of love and romance with men, but because she can no longer bear the burden that the emotional demands of her children make on her. In *The Awakening*, received ideas about the primary roles of women as wives and mothers which are still current today are questioned. The narrator makes no moral judgement, but merely shows how marriage and child rearing might become a prison for those who find from experience that this standard dual role is unsuited to their capacities. The 'awakening' in Edna's life is double – she is aroused to feelings of sexual lust, and to the fact that children for her are too much of a moral burden.

In *My Brilliant Career* (1901), the heroine, Sybylla Melvyn, who comes from the Australian 'bush' country, does not allow 'Fate' in the form of Harold Beecham to decide her career. She is not totally against marriage. But she concludes that Harold would not make a suitable partner for her, since she wants to become a writer and he refuses to take her vocation seriously. She tells him:

'If you had any sense, you'd have nothing to do with me . . . I am given to something which a man never pardons in a woman . . . I am given to writing stories, and literary people predict I will yet be an authoress.'

He laughed – his soft, rich laugh.

'That's just into my hand. I'd rather work all day than write the shortest letter; so if you will give me a hand occasionally, you can write as many yarns as you like. I'll give you a study, and send for a truck-load of writing-gear at once, if you like. . .'

No; I would not yield. He offered me everything – but control. He was a man who meant all he said. His were no idle promises on the spur of the moment. But no, no, no, no, he was not for me. My love must know, must have suffered, must understand . . . There was another to think of than myself, and that was Harold . . . to this man I would be as a two-edged sword in the hand of a novice – gashing his fingers at every turn, and eventually stabbing his honest heart.[13]

Central to this narrative is a critique of patriarchal hegemony which is epitomised in Sybylla's use of the word 'control'. At the same time, the narrator is caught up with the notion of 'romance' by which Sybylla is shown to be almost taken in. Sybylla enjoys her prettification by her aunt in order that she attract men such as Harold, even though she accepts no proposal of marriage.

Sybylla tries to escape the imprisonment of the role of helpmeet and child bearer by behaving like a boy in childhood and by seeking a career as a writer in adulthood. As a child her self-control is tested by her father cracking a whip around her; a similar testing occurs in her relationship with her putative lover, Harold. Symbolically she is being kept in her place as a woman by this parade of male dominance in the form of the whip (which, even in Australia, is usually reserved for horses). Sybylla herself learns to use a whip, and when Harold tries to kiss her at the point of their engagement, she slashes him across the face. We can read this episode either as a display of frigidity in Sybylla or as Sybylla's expression of rebellion against patriarchal restrictions.

As is demonstrated by Franklin's second novel, *My Career Goes Bung* (written in 1902, but first published in 1947), one of the major difficulties for women at the beginning of the twentieth century was an economic one: how to earn money if you sought sexual freedom by not getting married. Other women novelists, such as the American Edith Wharton, have centred a few novels on these kinds of personal and social problems which affect only women. If, for example, Lily Barton in *The House of Mirth* (1905) fails to marry well, she will have no means of support. Lily cannot attract a husband whom she could love and with means enough to suit her, but will not marry a poor man whom she loves. She turns to trimming hats for a living, is unsuccessful at that, and kills herself, because she sees no future without a loving man to support her. What the narrator reveals is the difficulty of fitting into society if you do not subscribe to the prevailing conventions for expressing sexuality. In Lily's world, people can flout sexual mores as long as they are not discovered. Wharton wrote during a time when those for women, partly because of the new methods of birth control, began to alter. This change led to a new freedom for women in sexual relationships outside marriage.

Whether Christina Stead is seen as an insider or outsider, her novels from the early 1930s onwards have explored and analysed women's sexuality in relation to their social and economic position. The emptiness of the lives of women who live off men is shown in novels such as *The Beauties and the Furies* (1936). Elvira, the heroine, leaves her London doctor–husband to go to Paris with her lover, Oliver:

> 'I've always been idle and useless,' mourned Elvira. 'It's true, I could have gone on to do something. I came first in things often at school. I got my B.A. What good did it do? I was born that way. Other women could have gone on and made a career. When Paul came along, I wanted him to love me but I didn't want to marry: I wanted to be myself, not a wife, with children. I wanted to do something creative: something – perhaps writing. I didn't want just to turn into a bad incubator. I didn't want to marry him, I just wanted to live platonically with him. But he wouldn't. It gave me a shock: I thought it was so gross of him. Afterwards, of course, I felt differently. I was a bad wife to him. Yes, I was. Everything I have ever done was bad and inefficient. I never had anything out of life that I should have had. I'm pretty, and I didn't have a good time. I'm intelligent, and I never did anything. I married, and I didn't even have a proper home with children. I ran away with a lover, and I'm miserable. And it's all my doing.'[14]

Yet Elvira is aware of what her main problem is: lack of independence, and being forced, because of choosing the social status of marriage, to be economically dependent on a man. She confides in her lover:

> 'It's degrading to be a woman, to have to bother about what people think, not to be able to provide for your child, to be dependent on men. If I'd kept on being secretary in that hospital, I should have been free, I should have had my job: now, he's taken me out of it, I've become a plaything; I'm no good. I can't even have my own child when I want it: it has to wait on circumstances. Do you think I like to pretend to be your wife when I'm not? . . . The real thought of the middle-class woman . . . is the problem of economic freedom and sexual freedom: they can't be attained at the same time. We are not free. The slave of the kitchen and bedroom.'[15]

In the ideological world of this novel, the attainment of economic freedom for women who are attracted by the possibility of sexual fulfilment and children seems impossible. And in the actual world of the 1980s, employed women with husband and children often endure a triple commitment: in kitchen, bedroom, *and* workplace.

In Stead's later novel, *For Love Alone* (1945), this theme of inequality between men and women, particularly in sexual relationships, is explored more fully. Teresa, the heroine, achieves sexual freedom at the expense of the old verities of fidelity and truthfulness. Teresa flees from the antipodean New World with its 'marriage sleep that lasted to the grave' in order to seek a 'great destiny' in the Old by going in for both sexual freedom and creative writing. In this novel, a mature woman is shown as needing to love freely wherever she finds love, even though society expects her to remain at least serially constant to one man:

> Woman had a power to achieve happiness . . . but in what way? Only by having the right to love. In the old days, the girls were married without love, for property, and nowadays they were forced to marry, of themselves, without knowing love, for wages. It was easy to see how upsetting it would be if women began to love freely where love came to them. An abyss would open in the principal shopping street of every town. But Teresa did not worry about her sisters. . .[16]

Nevertheless, despite this manifesto invoking freedom, Teresa shows compunction for her *de facto* husband, James Quick, and her concern for him prevents her from taking a lover permanently:

> 'He [Harry, her lover] won't come back, I know, and if he comes back I will never see him again,' said Teresa. 'I know that and I promise it to you now. I don't think chastity and monogamy and all that is necessary, but somehow – I don't want you to think I love you less.'[17]

Thus Teresa tempers free love with *realpolitik*.

Stead's creation, Letty Fox, represents the sexually buccaneering post-1945 young women of America. She is free of shibboleths about chastity, yet nevertheless is on the look-out for a husband. But in *Letty Fox: Her Luck* (1946, reprinted Virago, 1978), it is not only women who are hooked on romantic sexual love. In this extract, Phillip, Letty's uncle, bemoans his loveless existence:

> '. . . all those words, Shakespeare's sonnets, love songs, the weakest, worst lyrics in juke-boxes, to die for love, star-crossed lovers, all that, mean something to me; they are enough to give me heartache. I am still looking for love, after all my bitter experience. Experience so black and cruel, it is enough to kill a man, and yet, I long to be loved. If only you [Letty] and I could go away and love – I don't mean it, I mean if only – if

still – at my age, with what I know; you can't kill love in a man. That, too,
is driving me mad . . . I'll kill myself, Letty.'[18]

Phillip's suicide underlines the absurdity of any man or woman's
desire for a romantic love which is recognised even by Phillip as a
dream partly created by both high and pop cultures.

But, according to Letty, the phenomenon of sexual love is
constructed differently for women. She tells Cornelius, who already
has a wife and mistress as well as Letty for his lover:

> 'you don't know the first thing about women, which is, that when you live
> with them, they begin to love you. This is because they are more earthy
> and also more honest than you are. When they give their body, they give
> their heart and soul, too. Isn't that honest? It is men who whore! What
> are agreements? Agreements aren't written in flesh and blood. That's
> the only sort that can hold. With your pen on my papyrus, you see, you
> wrote something, you can't wash that out; you can't reason it away with
> your dry, feathery, insane Dutch reason.'[19]

Cornelius dislikes such plain-speaking, and dismisses her as his
lover. But Cornelius is just one of many men that Letty tries out as a
possible husband in her long search which she approaches as the
twentieth-century ritual it is:

> 'In other times, society regarded us as cattle or handsome house slaves;
> the ability to sell ourselves in any way we like is a step towards freedom;
> we are in just the same position as our Negro compatriots – and they
> would not go backwards to their miserable past. One must take the good
> with the bad. . .'[20]

So Letty's odyssey consists of discovering ways of attracting men in
order to marry one and live off him when she has children. When
she finally settles for her cousin, the multimillionaire, Bill van
Week, he is disinherited, but she sticks with him because she
appreciates his good qualities of decency and affection. Her efforts
to sell herself in marriage have served to sharpen her sensitivity to
goodness in men, so that we leave her ready with her 'freight' to
'cast off' because 'the journey [in marriage] has begun'.[21]

Although *Letty Fox: Her Luck* is set in New York towards the end
of the Second World War, in its characters' mores and expectations
this novel relates to any Western society from 1940 onwards.
Women today are often as much the sexual adventurers as men are,

at least in urban society. After marriage, such women might be aptly termed 'reformed rakes', which is Letty's term for herself. Marriage as an institution remains the most viable option for women at present if they desire children. That interim period between young adulthood and marriage is still often seen as merely a staging-post before life's marriage 'journey'. Letty's views are not those of Stead, nor indeed those of the narrator or 'implied author'. But the ideological stance of this novel, as portrayed through plotting and characterisation, lies paradoxically in the two premises that romantic love is illusory and that 'married love' of some kind is necessary for the fulfilment of some women.

In Jean Rhys's fiction, the male characters are the active moneyed participants of patriarchy and the female characters are the passive unmoneyed dependants. Her novels, apart from *Wide Sargasso Sea*, an historical work, were all published before the Second World War, the final one being *Good Morning Midnight* (1939). In *After Leaving Mr Mackenzie* (1930), for example, the heroine, Julia Martin, is 'very much afraid' of Mr Mackenzie, her former lover, and his lawyer:

> When she thought of the combination of Mr Mackenzie and Maître Legros, all sense of reality deserted her and it seemed to her that there were no limits at all to their joint powers of defeating and hurting her. Together the two perfectly represented organized society, in which she had no place and against which she had not a dog's chance.[22]

Julia is handicapped by her lack of training for any kind of skilled work, which makes her dependent on her ability to exploit her sexuality and to cadge money from men.

Sasha, the heroine of *Good Morning Midnight*, goes further along the sexual road of no return. She is ageing physically, afraid of loneliness, and sexually and financially dependent on whatever man she can get. But what can we expect of fictional – or, indeed, real-life – women who are not experienced in or educated for any mode of living in which to serve society except as sexual partners for men?

And another outsider, Canadian Margaret Atwood, in *The Edible Woman* (1969), satirises Western consumerism on two levels: that of well-packaged and well-advertised food and that of well-packaged and well-groomed women as purchasable objects for men. The two narrators, the heroine, Marian, and an unnamed third-person narrator, counterpoint various aspects of sexuality and marriage. We see the less-than-blissful marriage of Joe and Clara in the throes of persecution by their small children; Ainsley's reversal of her decision to have a child without marriage when she 'falls in love'; the engagement of Marian which does not survive her feeling of being owned by a man; and Duncan's wry use of women to meet his occasional need. The conclusion to this novel is ambivalent: the reader who prefers so-called 'happy' endings can envisage Marian and Duncan making a go of it together, and the realistic reader can imagine each of them maintaining his or her independence.

The Edible Woman works as a parody of the socialisation of late twentieth-century women into marriage partners: if the heroine is not willing to become a 'consumer' of 'feminine' objects and also be 'consumed' by some man in marriage, then she will be criticised for 'rejecting' her femininity. When Marian makes a cake which is in the form of a doll that symbolises femininity, and then eats it, her friend, Ainsley, looks upon this as Marian's demolishing of her womanhood. But this consumption of the superficial elements of life, as represented by the cake, allows Marian to free herself of her anorexic fears and to eat sensibly again. She, according to Duncan, has returned to so-called reality as a consumer. In *The Edible Woman* it is the institution of marriage itself which causes the evaporation of independent personality in both women *and* men. Women, despite their mothering role, become insubstantial, and men such as Clara's husband, Joe, are transformed into cogs in the patriarchal wheel.

Atwood's later novel, *Life Before Man* (1979), represents marriages which are breaking up and new ones in the process of formation. Women are shown as having enjoyable lives without the companionship of men, but the procreation of children, especially in the case of the paleontologist, Lesje, brings about change:

> A pregnant paleontologist is surely a contradiction in terms. Her business is the naming of bones, not the creation of flesh . . . It's hard to believe that such a negligible act of hers can have measurable consequences for other people, even such a small number of them.[23]

This characterisation of Lesje at least reveals a woman who is not marginal and who can live independently from men. By the conclusion of this novel, Lesje has not committed herself to her lover, Nate. And Elizabeth, Nate's former wife, has freed herself from her need of men: 'Suddenly Elizabeth feels, not lonely, but single, alone. She can't remember the last time anyone other than her children helped her to do something . . . paradise does not exist.'[24] In this novel, marriage is represented as no heaven, nor then is it hell: it is just a state of existence – one possibility among others.

Fiction, unless it is historical fiction, can either reflect the ideological mores of its period, or subvert those mores. Or, by presenting warring ideologies, some novels might do both at once. Fay Weldon's *The Heart of the Country* (1987), for example, satirises contemporary Western society which countenances adultery as 'a bit on the side' at the same time as legally treating sex outside marriage as grounds for divorce. And, as Sonia in this novel enquires, 'What does happen to the one in three women with children whose marriages end in divorce?'[25] The narrator leaves this general question unanswered. But it is a subject that has interested other women writers in the latter part of this century. Such writers now at times attempt to present women without men, very often after a failed marriage. Are these fiction-writers presenting received ideas about how women cannot live happily without men, or are they fictionalising a kind of new republic in which women are central and men are peripheral?

In Grace Bartram's recent work, *Peeling* (1986), which is set in Australia, the heroine Ally June Esterwood, loses her husband, Rowley, to another woman, Verna, in the first episode. In the remainder of this novel, the narrator explores her reactions to this loss in relation to the outside world as well as to her grown-up daughter, Jane. Ally goes through an initial period of denial of feelings of loss by reverting to an infantile state of passivity and greed which resembles catatonic schizophrenia. Once she acknowledges grief, she emerges from this torpor:

Grieving. She was *grieving*. Ally stopped crying, stood up and began pacing along the beach. She was in a state of grief! That's why she'd been behaving so strangely. As though after a death, she'd had to work her way through the shock of Rowley leaving her, of the breakdown of her marriage, such as it had been. She wasn't going crazy. She was simply mourning something lost.[26]

The words 'such as it had been' show Ally's acknowledgement that her marriage had been practically non-existent before Rowley left her. For years she had lived alone at her beach-house where he only visited her at weekends. But with his departure she now had no social *raison d'être*: 'she knew, with despair, that the company of others couldn't alter the basic problem, that she had nothing important or satisfying to do with her time'. Yet she had no more nor less to do with her time when Rowley had lived with her. The narrator makes no attempt to enlighten the reader about Ally's place in a politically patriarchal society. Throughout this novel, Ally remains economically dependent on Rowley, which implies a social and political naïveté on her part in regard to her relationship to men.

But if the narrator has a blind spot in relation to women's need to be independent of men either in marriage or out of it, Ally is shown as becoming knowledgeable about other areas which are central to feminist politics. She establishes a new life for herself after Rowley's desertion, although she continues to accept his money. She begins voluntary work in a women's 'refuge' where she assists in looking after women and children who have been driven from their homes by male violence. But Ally does not realise that her work is supported by Rowley in two ways – through the taxes he pays and through the money he gives her so that she can afford to do voluntary work:

'Have you got any idea how much public money is being poured into your goddamned refuges? [asks Rowley] Did you ever wonder how much tax I have to pay every year? Oh no of course you didn't. You've never been interested in my financial problems, have you? Never had to be, did you? The money's always been there for you. The government gets more out of every dollar I earn than I do and that's what they use to build your bloody welfare state, supporting women who can't be bothered to make a go of their marriages. . .'
'Jesus!' Ally shouted, 'I won't take any more money from you. I'll go on to a deserted wives' pension, you bastard.'
Rowley shouted as loudly, 'You will not! How dare you suggest such a thing? Do you think I haven't got any pride?[27]

Although feelings in women about divorce are universalised in *Peeling*, this episode can only be understood in terms of its Australian background. The stigma about receiving welfare benefits such as a 'deserted wives' pension' from the State is much greater than in some other Western countries, for example, Britain. The 'macho' Australian, Rowley, can only preserve his dignity by continuing to support Ally after he leaves her. But Ally does not question the fact that Rowley continues to give her the means with which to live even after their divorce. She has not worked since her marriage although she only had one child, Jane. Is she to remain a typical 'do-gooder' who helps others in order to have 'good' feelings? It seems so.

The narrator might have explored how Ally is perpetuating her powerlessness which began when she married. Independence for women is not just a matter of having some purpose in life, but is related to having a means of livelihood other than that of living off a man by doing housework and, perhaps, rearing one or two children. Wages for housework and child rearing might begin to solve the problems of wives, but in Ally's case, if she had been paid for her housework, she would not have earned much in the latter years of her marriage when she lived by herself at the beach. The sole purpose of Ally's voluntary work at the 'refuge' – in so far as we can infer this from what the narrator tells us – is that of exploring what she thinks and feels in relation to battered women. Ally in *Peeling*, despite the narrator's creation of a milieu which suggests that she is hard done by, remains a stereotype of the self-indulgent, socially parasitic woman who lives off a man.

Nevertheless, Ally is capable of casting off her stereotyped views about homosexuality when she learns from her daughter, Jane, that she is a lesbian, and that she is going to have a baby which she and her lesbian lover intend to bring up. But the fact that Ally accepts this relationship might be because the couple resemble a heterosexual one. In fact, the narrator presents their 'marriage' in language which is derivative of that long tradition of romance fiction about men and women:

> Jane's face turned ruddy in the warm light . . . 'I let myself go with it, because I had the feeling that if I didn't, I wouldn't get pregnant, you know? And if I got pregnant, I wanted it to be by someone I really liked. It wouldn't have seemed fair to the baby, otherwise. Marjorie, I thought you'd be pleased.'
>
> Marjorie sighed suddenly. 'It's OK.' She reached out and pulled Jane close. 'Look, it's all right. It's done now. It's going to be fine. It's what we both wanted, isn't it? You just made me feel funny, making decisions

that affect our future, screwing a guy I've never seen and not telling me
straightaway.'
  Jane said humbly, 'I felt nervous. I'm sorry.'
  Jane felt a little strange. What had just happened between them had
been very . . . married . . . almost as though Marjorie was a husband
who'd had unwelcome news of an unplanned pregnancy.[28]

These two women are portrayed as accepting their indebtedness to
a man who has unknowingly begot them a baby without their having
to acknowledge this fact to him. Their 'love' relationship is very different from that of a heterosexual couple, and it might have been
possible to suggest this through original language rather than giving
the reader a stock situation in clichés.
  In the 1960s and 1970s, philosophies of sexual liberation fostered
many kinds of so-called sexual freedoms. This phenomenon in the
USA is fictionalised in Lisa Alther's *Original Sins* (1981) in
which, through her characterisation of Emily, we experience vicariously the feelings of a lesbian 'coming out'. The heterosexual relationships in *Original Sins* are seen from the point of view
of what used to be known as a 'women's libber' and is now labelled
a 'feminist'. Here, for example, is part of the characterisation of
Raymond, who has been politicised in relation to capitalism and the
working class, but not in relation to his sexual domination of women:

> If only Thelma would argue with him, put him down sometimes,
> challenge him. As long as he fucked her, everything was fine with her.
> But Maria had cared about his political analysis, spoke his language.
> Thelma didn't have a clue what he was talking about . . . As he roared
> back to his house, Raymond realized he was alone again. Thelma was
> deserting him right when he needed her most. That was just about what
> he'd come to expect from women.[29]

Maria, Thelma – any female equivalent of Tom, Dick or Harry –
would suit Raymond, as long as she could meet his needs regardless
of her own. Of the four major characters in this novel, only Emily
becomes thoroughly politicised about the nature of women's lot:

> All the sweet sad brave women of Emily's youth . . . In every country,
> throughout history: Breasts sliced off, clitorises torn out, spears shoved
> up vaginas. By men. By the hirelings of the motherfuckers sitting in these
> pews looking smug and devout . . . There could be no exceptions. They
> all profited from each act performed by other men that kept women
> afraid and in their service.[30]

This passage represents Emily's fantasies after a member of her women's consciousness-raising group has been assaulted, raped and injured, but her list of crimes against women echoes passages in Simone de Beauvoir's historico-cultural-feminist study *The Second Sex*.

In any freethinking twentieth-century Western society, whether in life or as represented in fiction, freedom from ideological constraints is almost impossible. In the world of *Original Sins*, Emily has divested herself of one set of ideological shackles only to take on that new set which we label 'feminism':

> She longed to get back to New York and to Maria, who would hold her, touch her, and gently stroke life back into her numb body. And to the women's group, who would hear her out, taking on her sorrow as her own, restoring to her the strength and the will to continue the struggle on behalf of all the downtrodden women of the world. . .[31]

In these lines, the narrator implies that Emily has reached maturity in seizing on the 'correct' ideological viewpoint in relation to women. But perhaps the adoption of any ideological viewpoint, even of feminism, brings about a closed mind. Moreover, what Emily fails to note in her fictional world is that few women in the service of men want any change in their relationships with men.

Women collectively in the Western world need to redefine their place as individuals in society, rather than perpetually seeing themselves – because of their gender – as promoters of human relationships, both sexual and otherwise. In *Original Sins*, the narrator reveals how this preoccupation of women extends also to lesbian relationships. Maria, a minor character who is a lesbian, comments:

> 'Women have defined themselves through their relationships with men for so long that the temptation for lesbians is to continue to define ourselves through our relationships. I suppose to break out of this, we have to define ourselves through our work, or our politics, or our furniture or something.'[32]

So long as women in the actual world, and women writers in their partial mirrors of that world, continue to promulgate the idea that their importance lies in their ability to foster sexual and other relationships, then women's status in society will not change. Only when the majority of women begin to think that work is of equal importance, if indeed not more important, than the maintenance of relationships, will the remainder of society see us differently.

3

Work and 'brilliant' careers

Married women in fiction have been traditionally presented as non-career-making as well as prone to engaging in extramarital affairs. Molly Bloom in James Joyce's *Ulysses*, for example, is constructed characteristically as a women with the freedom and time to foster her sexual life outside marriage. Although she is a part-time singer, in her consciousness this work is represented as peripheral to her lust for men. Elvira, in Stead's *The Beauties and the Furies*, gives up her aspirations towards independent employment and settles for marriage with affairs on the side. Kate Chopin's *The Awakening*, Barbara Pym's *The Sweet Dove Died*, Margaret Drabble's *The Waterfall*, and A. S. Byatt's *Still Life* are among the legion of novels which give us bored housewives finding excitement in attracting and maintaining a lover outside marriage.

But what of unmarried 'career' women? We might discover feminine versions of *Lucky Jim* (1954), *Herzog* (1964) and *The History Man* (1975). Recently Joanna Russ, Valerie Miner and Alison Lurie have published novels which have women academics at their centre. But does this fiction subvert ideologies about women academics, or merely, like their male counterparts, subscribe to stereotypes about them? In Kingsley Amis's *Lucky Jim*, the lecturer anti-hero cannot live without a woman who is subordinate to him. The 'history man' in Malcolm Bradbury's novel, who seems to be mainly interested in women's sexual histories, has sexual relationships with women academics, but again only when he is in a dominating role. And Herzog's learned existence in Saul Bellow's novel is marked by the absence of female academics who are his equal: he depends on women, such as Ramona, the flower-shop proprietor, to service him in ways that suit him rather than her. All three novels reveal the egotistical male rampant.

Yet the lives of female academics in fiction by women tend also to be represented as alienated and unfruitful, if in a different way from representations of academic men. Esther in Joanna Russ's *On Strike Against God* (1980), for example, doesn't fit into her social milieu sexually and, because of her sexual difficulties, is not shown as enjoying the higher realms of teaching and thinking. Perhaps Esther might be seen as a lesbian 'Lucky Jim', but earlier fictional representations of career women in the world of teaching and learning have tended to be teachers and governesses, not lecturers and professors. These fictional teachers are serious thinkers, like Miriam in *Pilgrimage*, or feminist socialists, like Miss Kilman in *Mrs Dalloway*. Sarah Bourton, the headmistress in Winifred Holtby's *South Riding* (1936) has lovers, but nevertheless, at the end of the novel, looks forward to 'a serene old age' without sex. These career women are shown as of their period in having a choice between a sex life and a career, but not both together.

Is this concentration on teacher and governess heroines related to the novelists' own work experiences? Virginia Woolf comments on this question: 'That experience has a great influence on fiction is indisputable. The best part of Conrad's novels would be destroyed if it had been impossible for him to be a sailor.'[1] Some women writers have got around this lack of experience by seeking work in a field and class which are not their own, or by relying on historical sources for documentary material. And, as Keats observed, one does not have to become a 'sparrow' in order to 'take part in its existince [*sic*]'.[2] Virginia Woolf, despite her comment above, could construct characters who had roles other than those she had actually experienced, or even observed, herself. Yet the abundance of novels about teachers and governesses suggests that some women authors turned, for their subject matter, to their own experience of life.

Dorothy Richardson's first three novels, *Pointed Roofs* (1915), *Backwater* (1916) and *Honeycomb* (1917), in *Pilgrimage*, consist of a meticulous construction of a teacher–heroine who analyses each private moment. Miriam Henderson takes her first job as a teacher of English in a fee-paying boarding-school in Germany, then she teaches English Literature in a school of modest pretensions in North London and, finally, she becomes a governess with a wealthy family. These varieties of teaching experience allow the narrator to make social comments about the nature of education and its relationship to class. That Miriam is attuned to the nuances of her role as teacher in these different strata of society is evidenced in the following passage in which she compares her teaching of less well-off children in North London with her tutoring of two rich children:

> She had felt instinctively and at once that she could not use their lesson hours as opportunities for talking at large on general ideas, as she had done with the children in the Banbury Park School. Those children, the children of tradesmen most of them, could be allowed to take up the beginnings of ideas; 'ideals', the sense of modern reforms, they could be allowed to discuss anything from any point of view and take up attitudes and have opinions. The opportunity for discussion and for encouraging a definite attitude towards life was much greater in this quiet room with only the two children; but it would have been mean, Miriam felt, to take advantage of this opportunity; to be anything but strictly neutral and wary of generalizations. It would have been so easy. Probably a really 'conscientious' woman would have done it, have 'influenced' them, given the girl a bias in the direction of some life of devotion, hospital nursing or slum missionary work, and have filled the boy with ideas as to the essential superiority of 'Radicals'. Their minds were so soft and untouched . . . It ended in a conspiracy, they all sat masquerading, and finished their morning exhausted and relieved.[3]

Is Miriam revealed as a middle-class 'bourgeois' who looks down, to some extent, on tradespeople, and also defers too much to the feelings of the wealthy? Not completely. Her work as a teacher is difficult, partly because she is ill at ease when dealing with the nuances of a class-differentiated society of which she is almost too conscious to be 'conscientious' in trying to comment on it.

The preponderance of teachers among fictional women might be partly explained by the lack of choice of other professions for the educated woman. As Braybon and Summerfield show, in reality in Britain prior to the First World War, professional jobs in banking, the civil service, medicine, the law and so on were completely dominated by men. On the other hand, at that time,

> the number of women teaching in schools rose steadily. The 1870 Education Act led to an expansion in public elementary schools for working-class children, and more teachers were required . . . Numbers of high schools for girls increased as well. Initially these were private

schools, many of which were established by the Girls' Public Day School Company, but after 1902 local authorities began to set them up too. These offered more jobs for middle-class women, a growing number of whom were considering careers as well – not least because of the problem of 'surplus' women during the late nineteenth century. Emigration had led to an unbalanced sex ratio in some age groups, and a number of women realized that they could not depend on marriage as a career.[4]

Moreover, catching a husband depends not only on there being enough men available, but also on the girl's social charm and sexual attractiveness, qualities which are not always necessary in finding a job. Virginia Woolf's construction of the stereotyped feminist governess, Miss Kilman, who is Elizabeth Dalloway's tutor in *Mrs Dalloway* (1925) epitomises the female who is supposedly unattractive to men and therefore unlikely to marry. The narrator of this novel, in which Miss Kilman has a minor role, seems partly to condescend to women who do not meet conventional notions about the nature of beauty:

> Do her hair as she might, her forehead remained like an egg, bald, white. No clothes suited her. She might buy anything. And for a woman, of course, that meant never meeting the opposite sex. Never would she come first with anyone. Sometimes lately it had seemed to her that, except for Elizabeth [Dalloway], her food was all that she lived for; her comforts; her dinner; her tea; her hot-water bottle at night . . . However, she was Doris Kilman. She had her degree. She was a woman who had made her way in the world. Her knowledge of modern history was more than respectable.[5]

So much for the much-vaunted intellectual life, if no one loves or indeed even respects you. Through the eyes of the chief protagonist, Mrs Dalloway, Miss Kilman is seen as ugly, hateful and risible. Since the prevailing world-view in this novel is that of Mrs Dalloway, we are encouraged to accept Mrs Dalloway's valuation of her. Nevertheless, the narrator also presents Miss Kilman as opening Elizabeth's eyes to the possibility of a career and an intellectual life:

> Law, medicine, politics, all professions are open to women of your generation, said Miss Kilman. But for herself, her career was absolutely ruined, and was it her fault? . . . She [Elizabeth] liked people who were ill. And every profession is open to women of your generation, said Miss Kilman. So she might be a doctor. She might be a farmer. Animals are

often ill. She might own a thousand acres and have people under her. She would go and see them in their cottages . . . In short, she would like to have a profession. She would become a doctor, a farmer, possibly go into Parliament if she found it necessary . . .[6]

Here Elizabeth misconstrues Miss Kilman's ideals in order to identify with her father who is a member of parliament and representative of the 'patriarchy' in general. Her fantasy of visiting the farmworkers in their cottages implies a dream of authority and class superiority as much as of social service and intellectual creativity.

Yet Miss Kilman is not just a failed feminist. She is also constructed – in a way in which she has more force than Leonard Bast in *Howards End* – to represent a highly vindictive socialist viewpoint:

she did not envy women like Clarissa Dalloway; she pitied them . . . she stood on the soft carpet, looking at the old engraving of a little girl with a muff. With all this luxury going on, what hope was there for a better state of things? Instead of lying on a sofa – 'My mother is resting,' Elizabeth had said – she should have been in a factory; behind a counter; Mrs Dalloway and all the other fine ladies!

Nevertheless, the narrator of *Mrs Dalloway* makes her eponymous heroine more attractive than Miss Kilman, since, like the narrator in *Paradise Lost*, she is 'of the devil's party without knowing it' (William Blake, *Marriage of Heaven and Hell*). Miss Kilman's thoughts about redeploying rich idle women into the workforce in order that they might contribute their productive labour to society might be best-quality Fabian stuff via Bloomsbury, but it is not presented so as to win our liking for it or for Miss Kilman.

Historically, the teaching profession, along with that of nursing, was the most popular of professions for women, which perhaps also explains the popularity of this profession as a career for fictional women:

The number of women doctors increased during and after the First World War from 477 in 1911 to 2,580 in 1928. The number of women in the professional classes of the civil service was creeping up, too, though most of the 28,000 women employed there in 1939 were in the clerical grades. There were only fifty women in the better-paid and higher-status administrative grades in that year, and there were complaints that the selection procedures were stacked against women. Numbers in the professions which the Sex Discrimination (Removal) Act of 1919 had 'opened' to women were still pitiful. For example, there were a mere 82 women dentists, 21 women architects, and 10 women chartered accountants in 1928. The vast majority of professional women were either teachers or nurses, of whom there were 134,000 and 154,000 in 1938. Both teaching and nursing were considered 'good' careers for girls, although conditions could be rough under some employers, equal pay was non-existent, and the marriage bar, introduced into many public services as a cost-cutting exercise in 1922, presented work and marriage as incompatible alternatives.[8]

But why, given the fact that both teaching *and* nursing were considered '"good" careers' for girls, has there been no serious fiction about the lives of nurses?

Among the women novelists who centre on teacher–heroines, Winifred Holtby in *South Riding* (1936), constructs Sarah Bourton, who represents this new breed of careerist teacher. Unlike Miss Kilman, however, she arouses sexual love in men, but refuses to give up her ideals for 'love':

> She had been engaged to marry three different men . . . the third, an English Socialist member of Parliament, withdrew in alarm when he found her feminism to be not merely academic but insistent. That affair had shaken her badly, for she loved him. When he demanded that she should abandon, in his political interests, her profession gained at such considerable public cost and private effort, she offered to be his mistress instead of his wife and found that he was even more shocked by this suggestion than by her previous one that she should continue her teaching after marriage.[9]

Yet, despite this projection of an uncompromising feminist stance in the main character, feminist ideals are not sustained throughout this work. At the conclusion, feminism is closed off into a soft romanticism:

> In Mrs Beddows' smile was encouragement, gentle reproof, and a half-teasing affectionate admiration. Sarah, smiling back, felt all her new-found understanding of and love for the South Riding gathered up in her feeling for that small sturdy figure. She knew at last that she had found what she had been seeking. She saw that gaiety, that kindliness, that valour of the spirit, beckoning her on from a serene old age.[10]

Although no irony is apparent in the tone of this ending, we can only take Sarah's vision of Mrs Beddows in 'serene old age' as ironic in the light of earlier representations of Alderman Mrs Beddows as a do-gooder voluntary worker who enjoys unearned wealth.

How have women writers fictionalised the role of the artist which necessarily must touch upon their own aspirations? Do they conceive of the life of the artist as involving the renunciation of sexuality that is combined with marriage and the procreation of children? Tillie Olsen in *Silences* (1979) observes that gender affects the way in which girls conceive of their literary aspirations:

> some young women (others are already lost) maintain their ardent intention to write – fed indeed by the very glories of some of this literature that puts them down . . . High aim, and accomplishment toward it, discounted by the prevalent attitude that, as girls will probably marry (attitudes not applied to boys who will probably marry), writing is no more than an attainment of a dowry to be spent later according to the needs and circumstances within the true vocation: husband and family. The growing acceptance that going on will threaten other needs, to love and be loved. . .[11]

Tillie Olsen suggests here that the woman who wishes to devote her life to writing must necessarily, because of social constraints, give up the career of marriage and children. For women, the nurturing of husband and children is still a career, even though taking part in the work of a spouse and father is seen as a hobby for men, which they can take up or leave as they please.

This postulated dichotomy between marriage and writing is dismissed by some women. Buchi Emecheta, for example, has produced nine novels and an autobiography as well as five children, although she dispossessed herself of her husband in the process.

> As a child, I was brought up thinking that a happy home must be headed by a man, that we all had to make a home for him, not for ourselves, the women . . . During my marriage, Sylvester and I did not talk much in the evenings; we rowed most of the time. Yet I still felt the nagging guilt of incompleteness just because there was no man to talk to or serve or slave for at the end of the day. Now, suddenly, with more time on my hands to do exactly what I liked, that feeling was disappearing . . .
>
> I became so busy that I kept wondering how it was that only a few years back I had felt that to be a full human being, I had to be a mother, a wife, a worker and a wonder-woman. I now realized that what I was doing then was condemning myself to an earthly hell. Marriage is lovely when it works, but if it does not, should one condemn oneself? I stopped feeling guilty for being me.[12]

Emecheta gave up her roles of 'worker' and 'wife', restricting herself to writing and motherhood in order to enjoy her life.

Olsen suggests that 'portraits of the artist' by women are rare, and that the one she cites – Sylvia Plath's *The Bell Jar* – is 'inadequate' because the 'writer-being . . . is not portrayed'.[13] But such portraits of women artists, and even of the 'writer-being' are not so much 'rare' as overlooked. Miles Franklin's turn-of-the-century *My Brilliant Career* (1901) is one of these semi-autobiographical works. Franklin's heroine, Sybylla Melvyn, is constructed as possessing a strong urge towards literary production, despite considerable obstacles such as the accident of birth in the rural area of New South Wales at a period when the roles of wife and mother were considered more important for women than anything else they might aspire to in the way of vocation. Nevertheless, Sybylla is attributed with the insight that

> Marriage to me appeared the most horribly tied-down and unfair-to-women existence going. It would be from fair to middling if there was love; but I laughed at the idea of love, and determined never, never, never to marry . . . It came home to me as a great blow that it was only men who could take the world by its ears and conquer their fate, while women, metaphorically speaking, were forced to sit with tied hands and patiently suffer as the waves of fate tossed them hither and thither, battering and bruising without mercy.[14]

Yet, at times in this novel, Sybylla is shown as toying with the idea of marriage and a career as a writer:

> I believe in marriage – that is, I think it the most sensible and respectable arrangement for the replenishing of a nation which has yet been suggested. But marriage is a solemn issue of life. I was as suited for matrimony as any of the sex, but only with an exceptional helpmeet. . .[15]

Since Sybylla in this work is depicted as a sixteen-year-old, it is not surprising that she still subscribes to an adolescent dream of marriage that can be combined with a writing career.

In Franklin's subsequent *My Career Goes Bung* (written in 1902; first published 1946), the central female character is recognisably a slightly older Sybylla who deconstructs marriage and the adverse position in which this institution places women. But her putative lover, who resembles Harold Beecham in characterisation, is named Henry Beauchamp. Franklin might be trying to indicate that male responses to women are stereotyped in that whatever name they might have, men still try to possess women:

> 'You don't allow a woman any standing at all except by being the annexation of a man,' I [Sybylla] said.
> He [Henry] laughed in his large healthy way. 'Well, I did not arrange the world.'
> 'Yes, but you could help rearrange it,' I flashed, though I knew that among all the billions of men in the world there were few so just and brave that they would attempt any rearrangement that would lessen their top-dog self-confidence and loot . . .[16]

But if Sybylla is not going to become 'the annexation of a man' she has to find some other method of supporting herself. She realises that in marriage to Henry, just as in marriage to Harry in *My Brilliant Career*, her desire to become a writer will be annihilated:

> Henry once said that he would be jealous of my writing if it took up my spare time when he needed me. In short, my brain-children would be proscribed. I am weary of Henry's indulgent but inflexible assumption that my ideas are mere vivacity or girlish coquetry, which motherhood will extirpate. I can discern under the padded glove of spooniness the fixed determination to bend me to prescribed femaleness. Ah, no m'lord, the bait is not sufficiently enticing, nor does it entirely conceal the hook . . .[17]

In *My Career Goes Bung*, Franklin's narrator suggests that Sybylla's career will go 'bung' if she gets tied up sexually with men. The relationship between fictionalised autobiography and life is a complex one; nevertheless this title proved prophetic: not only was this novel not published for forty-four years because of fear of libel suits, since Franklin had based her characters on people she knew in Sydney, but also Franklin never wrote another novel as fresh and original as her first two. It was as if her 'brilliant' career in real life were epitomised in the title of her second novel.

Henry Handel Richardson's *The Getting of Wisdom* (1910) might also be described as a 'portrait of the artist' since part of the 'wisdom' its heroine, Laura Rambotham, learns at her private boarding-school for girls in Melbourne is that to lie in real life is a moral fault, but to fabricate convincingly in fiction is a strength. But nowhere has the idea of feminine devotion to the development of the artistic self been so well explored as in Willa Cather's *The Song of the Lark* (1915) and *Lucy Gayheart* (1935). In both these works, the heroines are so dedicated to their vocations as artists that at first they renounce marriage and children. This renunciation is presented as inducing conflicts between their artistic and sexual desires; for example, in *The Song of the Lark*, even though Thea Kronberg, the singer–heroine, wants to wake up 'every morning with the feeling that your life's your own',[18] she eventually succumbs to marriage with her long-term admirer, Ottenburg. And Lucy, the central character of *Lucy Gayheart*, is constructed, not as a dedicated artist, but as a musically gifted young woman who needs sexual love.

Lucy's first music teacher, Mr Auerbach, reiterates conventional clichés about love and marriage: 'In the musical profession there are many disappointments. A nice house and garden in a little town, with money enough not to worry, a family – that's the best life . . . You will learn that to live is the first thing.'[19] But 'to live' means different things to different people, and not every woman wants to settle for a bourgeois marriage which prevents her from exploring or expressing her talent. Lucy, after an abortive passion for the already-married singer, Clement Sebastian, for whom she works as an accompanist, is shocked by his death by drowning into realising that not even her joy in her musicianship represents all the possibilities of experience. She asserts that 'Life itself' was 'the sweetheart': 'It was like a lover waiting for her in distant cities – across the sea; drawing her, enticing her, weaving a spell over her'.[20] But her delight in this insight is cut short, since she dies in a drowning accident herself.

The underlying world-view of this novel is inherent in its suggestion that the artistic temperament itself might lead to non-fulfilment of the individual's talent. Music, painting and literature are produced, not God-given through mystical inspiration, but not everyone has talent. In the case of the fictional Lucy and her putative lover, Clement Sebastian, both musicians allow their emotional life to hold sway: Clement drowns in a boating accident which the narrator implies has been caused by his long-standing male accompanist, who is jealous of Lucy; and Lucy, when refused a lift by her former beau, Harry Gordon, unwittingly skates onto soft ice in an ill-temper and drowns. But Harry, the phlegmatic philistine, merely learns resignation from his loss of Lucy, whom he had loved: 'What was a man's "home town" . . . but the place where he had had disappointments and learnt to bear them?'[21] The life of the artist is passionate, intense . . . and short, but no judgements are made about the relationship between society and the artist, male or female.

Christina Stead's fictionalised woman writer in *Miss Herbert (The Suburban Wife)* (1976) is not a 'portrait of the artist': Eleanor Herbert is short on the skills of 'production' but long on re-doing other people's work. At her father's request, she revises his novel, *Brief Candle*, which they publish under their joint names. But after his death, in the hope of employment as a publisher's reader, she appropriates this novel as her own: ' "Well," said Eleanor, smiling (and she could not help a note of patronage), "I am a writer myself. I brought out *Brief Candle* a year or two ago. Published by Abbess and Prior, Ltd." '[22] As a publisher's reader, she is exploited, working long hours for low rates of pay. Subsequently, through the help of a seasoned journalist, Cope Pigsney, she becomes a successful 'woman of letters':

> She found it was quite easy to write for papers with a world reputation. The pay was small and slow to come; you might wait six months for four guineas, and through these literary papers were sifted all the struggling writers. Those who could stay the course were those who had a paying job, were university professors and the like. But for Eleanor, brought up to look upon literary London as Parnassus, to write for such papers was bliss. Though they might not publish her name, nor all she wrote, and though they paid her such small money, it was a great reward: alongside her, unknown to her, were some of the others working, not for money but for 'glory'.[23]

But this romantising about literary hack work is soon subverted in the form of Pigsney's wife's comment about her own journalism: 'Just a hack. I live at the bottom of Grub Street . . . where you grub in the garbage of literature for a living.'[24] Eleanor eventually succeeds at establishing herself as a literary agent, through which she helps others to see their work into print. This latter role conforms more to the stereotype of woman as midwife to the labours of others, which is consistent with received views. Is the prevailing set of ideas in this novel more than a repetition of current stereotypes? Perhaps the character of Miss Herbert is constructed so as to show that women who are left to support themselves will behave like similar untalented men who parasitically exploit the labour of others. Not that literary agents are all exploiters, but that Eleanor Herbert had aspirations towards literary creativity which she never pursued.

The documentation of the lives of skilled workers is rarely the subject of any fiction. Henry Green's *Living* (1929), which is mainly set in a Birmingham engineering works, and Walter Greenwood's *Love on the Dole* (1933) are exceptional in male fiction, but their novels are seldom considered as part of the 'Eng. Lit.' canon. In studies of 'modernism', Green's *Living* is as much overlooked as Richardson's *Pilgrimage*. And Nell Dunn's set of sketches in *Up the Junction* (1963) which encompass, among other things, factory-life for women, were only reprinted by Virago in 1988. Fiction about unskilled workers such as cleaners and dustmen is almost non-existent, apart from a few works such as Joan Riley's *Waiting in the Twilight* (1987) which dramatises the life of a West Indian cleaner in Britain. But even this heroine began as a skilled seamstress, and only became a cleaner as the result of a stroke.

In the nineteenth century, Elizabeth Gaskell had established the beginnings of a sub-genre which centred on the theme of the single working woman. In her short story, 'The Three Eras of Libbie Marsh' (1847), for example, Libbie is the unmarried and plain seamstress heroine who, in order that neither should feel unwanted, decides to live with the bereaved washerwoman whose crippled son Libbie had befriended. In some of her other stories of Victorian society, Gaskell portrays the problems of single women who have to support themselves.[25] In some of her novels, such as *Mary Barton* (1848), she shows the working conditions of men and women, in this instance in the Manchester mills. In *Ruth* (1853), she uncovers the plight of the unmarried working mother, and in *North and South* (1855), she explores, among other things, industrial relations and poverty among the mill-workers. The heroines of these novels, as well as those of *Sylvia's Lovers* (1863–4) and *Wives and Daughters* (1864–6), are not romanticised. These themes of working women *and* men, illegitimacy, celibacy in single working women, and close relationships between central female characters *without men* are still seldom the subject of fiction by women.

One of the few twentieth-century works of fiction which explores the plight of an unskilled single woman is Storm Jameson's 'A Day Off' (1933). The tale of the anonymous heroine, who is now the middle-aged mistress of George, is narrated in flashbacks through which the reader learns that she had started work in a cotton mill at the age of fifteen. On her first day, she had been humiliated by the authoritarian foreman:

> She found the place [the toilet] . . . When she came out the foreman from her room was waiting for her close to the door. He had his watch in his hand and he said sharply: 'You've been in there four and a half minutes. I was timing you. Don't do it again. I'm up to those tricks, see?'
> She looked at him and rushed back to the room.
> Big Kate saw that something was wrong. After a moment she came and stood by the girl, watching her movements. 'You c'n do that without moving your arm. See? Saves trouble – you don't want to kill yourself working for the ——s.' Her voice, warm and not loud – it slid itself through some crack in the deafening noise – poured an amazing relief through the girl's mind. She said nothing, but she felt less disgraced.[26]

In this passage, an older, more experienced woman had initiated her into a subversive attitude: to refer to the bosses in their own obscene coin, and to do the work to earn the money with the least possible expenditure of effort.

Very quickly the atmosphere and noise of the mill had affected her adversely:

> In a few months she was a changed creature. She held her own with the foreman and even invented a name for him that sent the others into paroxysms of rude laughter . . . one day she stood up on the table and danced, lifting her skirts. The men standing around in the yard crowded to the window and bawled their interest in the performance. She didn't care, not she. She cake-walked the length of the table, head back, her behind well out, elbows sawing the air in time to the steps.[27]

Thus she had achieved an ambiguous freedom from restraint, but at some cost to her inner world. This ambiguous freedom, in conjunction with the constant oppression of her spirit by the noise of the factory machines, had resulted in an erosion of her ego or will-power, and at seventeen she had 'let herself be seduced'. Her lover, who had promised marriage, never returned to Stavely, so that, in order to conceal the fact that she had been jilted, she travelled to London, ostensibly to join him, but actually to find work.

She worked in London as a maid, then took up with a German immigrant, Ernst, who also supported his legal wife at home. Ernst disappeared when war broke out with Germany in 1914, and she was unable to carry on his cafe on her own. She then lived off one man after another by selling sexual favours. By the conclusion, she had become so broken down that she stole a handbag from an elderly woman. George, her most recent lover, abandoned her, offering her a weekly allowance 'until she could get settled with something'. She realised that George's pay-off would soon cease, but nevertheless asserted, 'I'm not done for yet. I'm alive still'.[28] Now that she had become too old to interest men sexually, a patriarchal society had nothing to offer her. This parable about the dependent unskilled woman who must rely on male charity is relevant even today, particularly when social security payments depend upon the female payee not cohabiting with a man.

During the Second World War, women again engaged in supposedly male paid employment, as they had done during the First World War, only to suffer after 1945 a second postwar relegation to hearth and home. Gail Braybon and Penny Summerfield show us that 'the surprise and hostility with which women were greeted when they were once again moved on to new jobs in 1939–45 do not suggest that the First World War had led to permanent changes'.[29] As the Chief Inspector of Factories reported in 1919, 'interesting work is being taken out of their [women's] hands, and they are steadily being forced back into the routine of their hitherto normal occupations'.[30] In fact, according to Braybon and Summerfield, women this century have been continually 'confined within the "cage" of domesticity and low esteem at home and at work',[31] apart from the brief periods of the First and Second World Wars.

Women's skilled and unskilled work during the two world wars has rarely been the subject of fiction, except for a few works such as Stevie Davies's historical novel, *Boy Blue* (1987), which is set during and after the Second World War. Lilian, who has not married, describes to her niece, Florence, how she was 'pushed out' of so-called male jobs after the war:

'I've had some jobs too in my time, I can tell you. But the end of the war finished all that. The men were demobbed and the women were pushed out of the good jobs. We'd been called up and directed into work, you see, but it was on what they liked to call a voluntary principle – so I took up all sorts of trades – land girl, coalman, plumber, fireman, I was all those – and then when I got fed up with it, I just chucked it in and looked for something else. Oh yes, the war was a great time; the happiest days of my life.'

The end of the war had not only put a stop to Lilian's professional adventures; it had soured her temper and accentuated the bitter streak in her nature, by stamping her a spinster and nothing more. She found herself devalued by the returning armies of young men who swamped the labour market. Domesticity and child rearing were recommended for women, now that they had done their bit. '*I* don't intend to end my life a clucking hen laying eggs in a hen coop,' Lilian had said to anyone who would listen . . . She took over a couple of allotments, and started to cultivate them . . . she sold produce privately, and finally opened a market garden.[32]

Lilian resourcefully finds a niche for herself in which her talent for what most people consider to be male work will be tolerated. But she thinks that she 'is just a joke to people – half woman, half man – bit of a dinosaur, good for work, surplus to requirements. Marital status: Spinster. Status: Nil.'[33] The status of the spinster is still low, unless she stands out in one of the arts: acting, dancing, writing, or performing on television.

The plight of the unskilled working 'spinster' has rarely been the subject of British fiction during even the latter part of this century. Nell Dunn's *Up the Junction* (1963), which comprises a series of inter-related stories about the lives of young unmarried women at work and in their relationships with young men, is one of the few exceptional works on this subject. One of these sketches, for example, deals with women at work in a chocolate factory:

I call Ruby. 'Could you come over here a minute please?'
    'Listen to that. We've got to take her in hand – teach her how to speak. You say, "Rube, fuck you, get over here, mate!"'[34]

Streetwise language and bravado are imprinted on a conventionally ladylike young woman, as if to send up and oppose the artificiality of the conventionally feminine.

A dominant feature of late nineteenth- and early twentieth-century Australian life and literature is that of a rough kind of egalitarianism, which is perhaps symbolised by the 1880s and 1890s ideal of 'mateship' between men. One ironic consequence of the idea that one person is as good as another is the preponderance of outspoken women among important writers of serious fiction in

Australia in the early and mid-twentieth century. Such women writers – even if they occasionally hid their gender behind male pseudonyms – emerged from a society which allowed more free-floating movement across and around the partly make-it-up-as-you-go social scale than was possible in Britain. But this initial possibility of social and sexual egalitarianism in Australia, as in Canada and the USA, has been gradually eroded by a vulgarly class-creating consciousness of money.

Kylie Tennant's first novel, *Tiburon* (1935), describes the egalitarian working world of the 'travellers' – out-of-work men and women who toured around seeking paid employment in outback Australia in the 1930s depression – as well as that of the schoolteacher, Jessica Daunt. The plot of this novel centres on a strike which resulted in unexpected freedoms for women who were only housewives:

> So the strikers had meetings, and their wives ran the two soup-kitchens for the travellers and the single men. The wives were still having a wonderful time. Almost as one woman they wanted the strike to go on, because they were away for once from the drudgery of the home, mixing with other women, without anyone to comment on unswept floors and undone washing.[35]

But, ironically, for Jessica, her one year of teaching at Tiburon pushes her into marriage as an escape from the difficulties of her social life there:

> 'I can't go on teaching,' she told herself. 'I won't, not if I have to beg in the gutter. Her mind felt sick as she thought of Tiburon . . . She tried to think of something more pleasant, the prospect of being met at the station by her family. Perhaps Jeff Hardwick might be there . . . Was he still keen on her, she wondered. Would he ask her to marry him again. . .[36]

Predictably, not long afterwards she announces her engagement. She is saved from the discomforts of class prejudice in Tiburon only to enter that very state which the strikers' wives find imprisons them.

One of Tennant's subsequent heroines, Mallee Herrick, a migratory apiarist, evades the institution of marriage in order to become a successful beekeeper – an occupation which is not usually followed by women, especially women operating on their own. Mallee is presented as a composite human being who, despite her gender, has a lot in common with men. At first she tries to maintain her own hives with male assistance, but without those same men importuning her for sexual favours. But, not surprisingly, given common male assumptions and fantasies about women, Herrick finds it impossible to be friendly in a non-sexual way with men:

> I quite agreed with all the people . . . who had warned me that it was not possible to be friends with men. The mistake I had been making all my life is that I always thought you could. I like friends, I like being friends with men, but only a fool will go on trying to do the impossible. No, men and women should live in separate worlds with the doors locked between them. Centuries of training are needed before men and women can be civilized to the stage where they can be friends. I don't mean equals. I don't care who is better than whom. I mean friends.[37]

In fact, she is only able to escape the predatory and three-timing Blaze Muirden by taking her bees to another state and working independently of him and other men:

> The smell of honey and the smell of smoke – the trucks roaring away for hundreds of miles carrying the bees to blossom. This time – oh, this time I'll be on my own.[38]

This is a remarkably anti-romantic conclusion in which the heroine does not get her man – in fact, does not want a man.

Even after the turn of the century, girls whose parents could afford to keep them if they did not marry were educated to become 'ladies' and not to seek paid employment. But, since more women in the latter part of this century now marry, have children *and* continue to work in paid employment, we might expect more fiction which represents women engaged in such a threefold career. The Australian novelist, Katherine Susannah Prichard, provides an early model for such writing: she shows how paid employment, apart from, or as well as, child nurturing and housework, can be essential to any woman, whatever her sexual life and its consequences. Sally Gough, her central character in her postwar goldfields trilogy – *The Roaring Nineties* (1946), *Golden Miles* (1948) and *Winged Seeds* (1950) – is impelled to work, not only to support herself, but also to gain the economic power that a woman needs within her marriage as well as *vis-à-vis* her neighbours:

She was loth to look at Morris [her husband] except through the romantic glamour with which she had enveloped him when they ran away together and were married; but an instinct stirred, shrewd, critical, and realistic . . . If Morris was like that: if he was lazy, selfish, unscrupulous about money, and his passion for her had faded, she must manage her life without depending on him: be prepared to manage him also. She had no intention of allowing him to drift and forget his obligations as he had been doing. Oh no! And she was not going to allow him to use her as he had done. Her life with Morris was going to be a partnership in which her clear brain and energy should have a chance. She would not fail in her duty to him; but he must also realize her right to a policy in their affairs.[39]

Strong stuff for a female character at the turn of the century, or for the majority of readers in the 1940s when these books first appeared.

Later, when Morris is away prospecting for gold, Sally, in order to support herself, opens a dining-room at Hannans for the miners living there: 'Her grit and energy were amazing. Thin as a rat, but always sprightly, she contrived to make a success of her dining-room and impress everybody by her good spirits.' Consequently, she was treated as an equal by the miners, so much so that she immediately identified herself with their political struggles:

She had lived and worked among prospectors and miners for so long: been on the same footing with them as a woman earning her living: knew so well the hardships of their lives, that she seemed to have adopted their point of view as a matter of course.[40]

In addition to bearing and rearing four sons, Sally eventually takes on the management of her own boarding-house in order to supplement Morris's uncertain income as an undertaker.

Prichard invented a variety of female characters who each had a very different kind of work. In order to achieve verisimilitude in her mid-career social realism, and a documentary quality in her naturalistic last novels, she either visited (as she did for the goldfields trilogy) or worked in (as she did for the circus novel) the environment in which she set her characters. Harry Heseltine observes about Prichard's preoccupation with different kinds of paid employment, 'At one level, her novels of the twenties and thirties provide a series of travelogues depicting a wide variety of occupations.'[41] But he does not analyse Prichard's interest in women's roles in those various industries and occupations.

Prichard, in consistently portraying women whose work is just as important as their relationships, is innovatory. Few of her female contemporaries in fiction-writing have so convincingly and continuously evoked the lives of women who, in addition to being wives and mothers, also work in semi-skilled, skilled or professional jobs. In *The Black Opal* (1921), the former professional singer, Sophie Rouminof, gets married, but is also shown developing her skill at polishing opals to make a living. In *Haxby's Circus* (1930), for which she had spent three months working in Wirth's travelling circus, she constructs Gina Haxby, a woman who becomes emancipated like herself. Gina is the daughter of a patriarchal circus ringmaster–proprietor, and, when she is disabled from a fall as a bareback rider, she becomes the circus drudge. But she fights back to become manager–owner, and finally also the clown:

> She seemed happiest really when, in her clown's dress, made-up with plastered face and rouged mouth, she waddled into the ring and tumbled about, making herself grotesque and hideous, to get the brittle crashing merriment of the crowd that could hurt her no more.[42]

Gina's emancipation from both her injury and her domineering father can be seen perhaps as an allegory for the progress of the free woman, who pays a price for claiming equality with men in their circus of life.

If women fiction-writers during the earlier part of this century have seldom engaged with the subject of women's work of the unskilled or semi-skilled kind, they have also not fictionalised to any great extent the professional work of women technicians, lawyers, doctors, scientists and so on. Only in the 1970s and 1980s has much fiction about the problems of women at work begun to appear. Zoe Fairbairns in *Closing* (1987), for example, centres on the lives of saleswomen, and in Michèle Roberts' *The Book of Mrs Noah* (1987), the eponymous heroine fantasises a different working existence from that of devoted wife.

Yet fiction which presents women in traditional roles is still paramount. Deborah Moggach's *Close to Home* (1979), for example, fictionalises a stereotypical housewife, Kate, with two infants and a civil servant husband who is often away in Brussels. A former secretary, she has no interests of her own apart from her children. Consequently, she can think of no way of relieving the pressures of caring for two infants except by encouraging sexual overtures from her next door neighbour, Sam. When this relationship is aborted by her oldest child crying out, she settles for a week, child free, with her husband in Paris, in the hope that this change will relieve her boredom. Yet some women in real life pursue further study, or a few hours' paid employment, in those three or four hours when their babies are asleep or in a playgroup. Fictional Kate, however, has no such ambition.

Jetta, another central female character, is constructed as a competent psychiatrist and breadwinner who has little understanding of her husband and daughter. Moreover, Kate is presented as endearing and Jetta as unlikable, which suggests this novel's underlying ideology: women should concentrate their emotions on their families and not their paid employment. As long as women readers continue to identify with characters like Kate, no change in women's roles – or men's for that matter – can be expected. But in what other ways have mothers and children been fictionalised? Are there other possibilities for married and unmarried women with children apart from resignation and self-sacrifice?

4

Mothers and children

Masculine responses in fiction to the gestation and delivery of babies are few. William Blake, however, in 'Infant Sorrow' (*Songs of Experience*, 1794), gives a lyrical representation of childbirth from the point of view of the baby. The emergence from secure womb to 'dangerous world'; the travails of the mother; the emotionality of the father; the feeling of being circumscribed by restrictive clothing; the sulking upon the 'mother's breast' – Blake encapsulates what the psychoanalyst Carl Rogers called the 'birth trauma'. But the word 'trauma' – 'emotional shock' (*The Concise Oxford Dictionary*) – exaggerates what is after all only a stage in growth.

The act of giving birth is not featured in Molly Bloom's stream of consciousness in Joyce's *Ulysses*, although other aspects of motherhood are included. In D. H. Lawrence's *Sons and Lovers* (1913), the narrator skirts around the actual moment of birth:

> She [Mrs Morel] was very ill when her children were born.
> 'What is it?' she asked, feeling sick to death.
> 'A boy.'
> And she took consolation in that. The thought of being the mother of men was warming to her heart.[1]

Lawrence's male chauvinism here is on a par with his ignorance of childbirth. The usually arduous process of labour and giving birth can be painful and in the past has often resulted in a dangerous debility, but childbirth itself has never been conceived of as an illness.

In Lawrence's later novel, *The Rainbow* (1915), the birth of Lydia's first child is presented from the point of view of the new father, Tom Brangwen:

> He started. There was the sound of the owls – the moaning of the woman [Lydia, who is in labour]. What an uncanny sound! It was not human – at least to a man . . . She was beautiful to him – but it was not human. He had a dread of her as she lay there. What had she to do with him? She was other than himself.
>
> Something made him go and touch her fingers that were still grasped on the sheet. Her brown–grey eyes opened and looked at him. She did not know him as himself. But she knew him as the man. She looked at him as a woman in childbirth looks at the man who begot the child in her: an impersonal look, in the extreme hour, female to male. Her eyes closed again. A great scalding peace went over him, burning his heart and his entrails, passing off into the infinite.
>
> When her pains began afresh, tearing her, he turned aside, and could not look. But his heart in torture was at peace, his bowels were glad. He went downstairs . . .[2]

To Tom Brangwen, Lydia is 'other than himself'. Here the narrator epitomises what de Beauvoir was caustically to criticise: how throughout Western history woman has been viewed by man as less than human, sharing few of his own 'higher' capacities or faculties. The act of giving birth is seen as so quintessentially female that Lawrence's male protagonist is portrayed as being unable to empathise with the feelings of the mother about the delivery of the child he engendered.

Are there any fictional contraction-by-contraction accounts of childbirth, or are all such descriptions couched in nebulous terms such as 'moans' and 'pains'? The description of the delivery of Martha Quest's first baby in Doris Lessing's *A Proper Marriage* (1965) is conveyed from Martha's point of view, which gives the proceedings a ring of authenticity. What is noteworthy is Martha's feelings of loss of control over her body:

> And behold, Martha, that free spirit, understood from the exquisite shore of complete, empty non-sensation that she had been groaning out 'Mother, Mother, Mother!' Without a flicker of feeling in any part of her body, she felt the tears of failure roll down her face; and looked up through them to see the pink nurse looking down at her with unmistakable disappointment.[3]

What seems natural – to remember one's own mother and desire her help during labour – is treated as weakness by both Martha and her nurse. One might expect a representative of the authoritarian regime of a hospital to be constructed so as to disapprove of a show of feeling. But the narrator implies also that Martha's crying out *is* weakness in a 'free spirit'. Such repression of feeling is part of a general societal attitude to the display of emotion: feeling is assumed to be irrational and unacceptable, particularly when displayed by men or educated women.

Moreover, when her baby is finally delivered, Martha is prevented from seeing her new-born for twenty-four hours. This is another of those regulations brought about by a society which is dominated by male pseudo-scientific shibboleths. But such shibboleths change, according to the kind as much as the quality of research that is being undertaken. Research itself is subject to the forces of ideological belief at any given period.

Until recently, even in fiction by women, childbirth and the care of the new-born did not feature much in novels. But Elizabeth Baines's *The Birth Machine* (1983) is coloured by the late 1960s and early 1970s swing towards natural childbirth. Her narrator implies criticism of the way in which Zelda, the heroine, has been trapped in the mechanistic process of a 'hi-tech' birth. Her experience of an induced birth is presented in free indirect discourse; that is, the narrator, in an impersonal voice, gives us Zelda's internal responses to outward events:

> The head smashes down through the bag of her abdomen. It won't come. It won't come out. Skull like a turnip, the enormous great big turnip that the farmer couldn't pull from the cold black earth. He pulled and pulled, but it wouldn't come up. The farmer called his wife. Sister calls Doctor. Doctor hears, Doctor sees. 'Foetal distress,' says Doctor; *foetal distress*, said the textbook in its outdated type on good old-fashioned paper; 'Foetal distress,' calls the nurse. Sister calls the hospital porter. The farmer's wife called the boy. The doctor raises a syringe and plunges the needle into Zelda's arm.[4]

Through this analogy with the folktale 'The Enormous Turnip', the narrator links Zelda's adult experience with her childhood. Zelda has a Caesarean section; her fantasy life, which has begun to overwhelm her with a mixture of past recollections and responses to the present, leads her after the birth to lose touch momentarily with reality. She is prescribed drugs for her supposed psychosis, but this clinical treatment obscures her need to see her baby:

> A nurse enters, talking over her shoulder. A doctor replies: 'No, it's OK, no problem, we'll give her something stronger. We'll get her through today, it doesn't matter if she's out, she's not feeding, is she?'
> A needle sinks into her arm.
> Who said that? Who said 'No'? 'No, she's not feeding'? What do they mean? Do they mean not eating? Not feeding. Feeding what? The baby. They mean the baby . . .
> 'Nurse, nurse that's not right, I want to feed my baby.'
> The water surges. She falls back. How could she, how silly, how could she ever get the nipple in?[5]

Because Zelda has not been permitted to see her baby, she fantasises that her offspring has been born without a mouth. Her paranoia is related partly to her childhood experience of discovering the body of a murdered child. But her loss of contact with the 'real' world stems mainly from her feelings about the 'convenience induction' which was rigged up by her doctor husband and his professor to suit themselves. She realises that she is under an authoritarian regime dominated by the male medical profession which includes her own husband:

> She hears them coming along the corridor, their voices reverent and low, the givers of life according to their own strict patterns. False patterns. Their gods are false: their stiff patterns can fail them. Death can leap up from the depths, gobbling, jump back into the machine; electric grids across the land, sustenance and life meted out in geometric patterns: the lights could go out, the machines fail at any moment . . .[6]

Zelda decides to defeat the mechanised 'system' by disappearing with her baby. Zelda's final destination with her child is not specified, so that the ending remains open to interpretation. Throughout this novel, however, Zelda's puerperal psychosis is shown to be explicable in the light of her reactions to the highly clinical treatment she receives at the maternity hospital where she has her baby.

But what about the process of mothering after the baby is born? To begin with, does fictional mothering still incorporate the easy-to-believe myth that the natural mother is the most suitable person to look after her own children? Since Bowlby tried to give this old assumption scientific credence in *Child Care and the Growth of Love* in 1953, this traditional belief has been especially hard to modify, even though Bowlby himself revised his theory that a child would become emotionally damaged if the natural mother did not care for it. He subsequently stated that a long-term mother substitute could be as good for a child as his or her natural mother. But, as Dorothy Dinnerstein records:

> . . . most of us go on feeling that the mother–child tie is in some real sense sacred: whatever else it may be, it is clearly the most fundamental, universal, biologically sturdy tie we have. To conserve the integrity of this tie, many people would argue, some minimal asymmetry in the sexual prerogatives of men and women – especially if hedged about by more humane laws and customs – may be a reasonable price to pay . . .
>
> What makes Motherhood reliable is that the erotic flow between the child and its female parent is primed by a set of powerful postpartum mechanisms, mechanisms which prompt not only women, but also simpler she-mammals, to nurture and protect their young. What makes Motherhood monstrous, atomistic, is that we force these primitive biological underpinnings – which are neither specifically human nor designed to do more than guarantee the brute survival of the newborn – to carry a peculiarly human, and wildly disproportionate psychological weight.[7]

And it is this 'psychological weight' that women find hardest to combine with the attractions and responsibilities of a career.

But Dinnerstein goes further. She suggests that this kind of all-embracing mothering, which splits off consciousness of the father in children, inhibits children's emotional maturing:

> Motherhood . . . gives us boys who will grow reliably into childish men, unsure of their grasp on life's primitive realities. And it gives us girls who will grow reliably into childish women, unsure of their right to full worldly adult status.[8]

Dinnerstein's solution is that both parents should become 'first' parents, that is, they should both care for the new-born infant equally.

Novels in which mothers are the 'first parent' are common in fiction by men. D. H. Lawrence's *Sons and Lovers* (1913) reflects in Mrs Morel an image of the kind of mother whose love for her fav-oured son borders on the incestuous and has the effect of crippling his sexual engagement with women of his own age. Stephen Dedalus's

mother in Joyce's *Portrait of the Artist as a Young Man* (1916) and
Ulysses (1922) is also portrayed as a possessive character, but her
effect works on her son's spiritual rather than his emotional life. In
both Lawrence's and Joyce's work, the maternal is an aspect of
existence which the sons are impelled to disavow. On the other
hand, the father in these novels is a weak and despised figure who is
given to drink.

An intriguing contrast to this kind of male perception of the
maternal is discoverable in novels from that same early twentieth-
century period. In Kate Chopin's *The Awakening* (1899), for
example, the heroine, Edna Pontellier, at first leaves her children
with her mother so that she, Edna, can live by herself in New
Orleans. She comes to recognise, however, that society has bound
her to her children, and prefers to let herself drown rather than face
a commitment for life to them. The narrator presents Edna's
inability to 'mother' in a sympathetic light, and we are shocked into
realising that not every woman's fulfilment of a biological urge to
procreate is succeeded by an impulse to nurture.

Edith Wharton's *The Mother's Recompense* (1925) is one of the
few twentieth-century novels which subverts the idea of a 'sacred'
bond between mother and child. In this work, the story-line shatters
the myth that motherhood is an attribute of all women who have
become biological mothers. Through flashbacks, the narrator
reveals how 44-year-old Kate Clephane abandoned her 3-year-old
daughter in order to fend off the boredom of marriage:

> 'lost' was the euphemism she had invented . . . because a mother
> couldn't confess, even to her most secret self, that she had willingly
> deserted her child. Yet that was what she had done; and now her
> thoughts, shrinking and shivering, were being forced back upon the fact.
> She had left Anne when Anne was a baby of three; left her with a
> dreadful pang, a rending of the inmost fibres, and yet a sense of
> unutterable relief, because to do so was to escape from the oppression of
> her married life . . .[9]

She had not run off because she loved another man, but merely
because she could not stand her husband's 'self-approval and
unperceivingness'. In order to escape him, she took up with a
known rake. When this affair was soon over, neither her husband
nor her mother-in-law would allow her to see her daughter again.

Kate Clephane drifted into a bohemian life on the Riviera where she had an affair with a younger man, Chris. Kate's daughter wanted contact with her mother upon the death of her father, and Kate returned to New York. Kate tried to redeem herself in the eyes of her child, but, in a highly contrived plot, Chris, Kate's former lover, had become her daughter's unofficial fiancé. Kate could not bring herself to reveal her former liaison with her daughter's fiancé and subsequent husband, and returned to the Riviera alone. Thus the mother in this instance was not recompensed for her early abandonment of her daughter, because, as the narrator implies very indirectly, she had led an unconventional and, for that era, an immoral life. Thus, the title is ironic, and the work as a whole supports the notion that deserting your children will lead to unhappiness.

The narrator in Jameson's trilogy, *Mirror in Darkness*, also implies that desertion of your child will lead to misery. The main character, Hervey Russell, in order to take up a career as an advertising copywriter in London, pays another woman in Yorkshire to look after her pre-school age son:

> She [Hervey] was tired but at first could not sleep for thinking of her baby. This child, who was three years old, and very beautiful, she had left in Yorkshire with a lady trained in the care of young children. The more she considered in her mind the perfections of this lady, the less comforted she was and scarcely able to bear being parted from him. What would he think and feel when, falling asleep in a strange room, he woke to find it stranger by daylight, and the door opening, and looking round for his mother, Miss Holland came in?[10]

Here the narrator, through her characterisation of Hervey, epitomises one of the central problems of motherhood. Although we might intellectually agree with Dorothy Dinnerstein that our responses to the needs of babies are biologically determined, this recognition does not do away with the emotions involved. Dinnerstein would of course suggest that the child's father should take some part in the nurturing of the child he begot, but fathers' hormonal responses are not geared, in life or in fiction, towards the demands of young babies and toddlers. Moreover, other essential responses that are needed in the nurture of infants must, in fathers even more than in mothers, be fostered and learned. And in this fictional instance, Hervey is separated from her husband although she continues to have a tenuous relationship with him.

In this realistic trilogy, this mother–child relationship is presented only from the mother's point of view, which restricts any comprehensive exploration of the child's feelings. In fact, in all the episodes in these three novels in which both children and adults participate, the children are invariably seen through adult female eyes. This blinkering of viewpoint does not allow the narrator to explore the child's reactions in order to give a moral perspective on the child's lack of power over his environment. Hervey does not talk about the proposed change with her son, nor is the introduction to the mother substitute undertaken gradually. The abruptness of Hervey's departure suggests a desire to mitigate her feelings of loss, which nevertheless overwhelm her later. One cannot propose that a novel published in the 1930s anticipate post-Second World War psychological discoveries about the need to make changes in a child's life slowly. But we might expect the narrator to make imaginative exploration of the subject of children's feelings when she enters into all sides of other questions, for example, the rights and wrongs of the 1926 General Strike.

In order to get over her loss of her son, Hervey deliberately represses her feelings about him, and only visits him when her guilt provokes her to do so. She tries to obliterate her responses to her son because she wants to pursue a career:

> Her wish to see and touch her son overcame her. She felt that she would cry, and pretended to drink her coffee, holding the cup at her mouth; her throat was rigid.
> Without thinking, she knew she would not go back. She was too dissatisfied, possessed by a devil of energy and ambition. At the least notion of giving up it sprang in her; she could not go back to Yorkshire, to become nothing, unknown. She had to have something to show.
> I should have no money, she thought, her mind turning from Richard to Richard's father . . . If he had work, between them they could contrive to live decently and have Richard with them. That's not a great deal to ask of him, she thought, with growing anger.[11]

This passage encapsulates one of the problems for any woman who seeks to engage in a career in a way that is similar to that of a man: who will take on the care of her children? If she can afford to pay someone else to do this work, will her children suffer, and will she herself suffer emotionally? When Tillie Olsen describes 'silences' enjoined on women by the pressures on them to perform domestic and child care duties, is she intimating that in some way women who are talented writers and artists should be freed from such burdens?

In her actual life, Storm Jameson faced this problem which she fictionalised in her characterisation of Hervey Russell. In her autobiographical *Journey from the North*, vol. 1 (1969), she describes how she left her three-year-old son, Bill, in the care of a paid, trained mother substitute, in order that she could take up a career in London:

> To give up my child in return for four pounds a week in an advertising office was plain madness, a folly for which there was no rag of excuse . . . I could have said – it would be true – that I felt responsible, solely responsible for our future. Justly or unjustly, I was quite certain now that K [her husband] would never do anything, for himself or us. I read his few letters with an eye that saw only their levity and what my grandfather would have called bombast. He has the mind, I thought cruelly, of a precocious schoolboy . . . My poverty and insecurity were a torment, and my blind wish was to do the best I could for my son. (That this did not necessarily involve having money did not brush a mind haunted by too many hard-headed ghosts.) By keeping mum about my ambition, boredom, restlessnes, I could make out an excellent case for myself. Any sensible jury would applaud it, and it would be a lie . . .[12]

Elsewhere, Jameson asserts that in *Journey from the North* she is striving towards objective truth – 'a book in which I am trying to write without lying' – whereas in her trilogy, *Mirror in Darkness*, she could fictionalise these events as much as she liked, so long as, in the realistic mode she had chosen, what she wrote was convincing. What is interesting about the mother–child relationship as it is fictionalised in the one text and 'objectively' related in the other, is that both texts carry the implication that mothers are not able to leave their children in order to pursue careers without feeling uncontrollable remorse and guilt.

The real-life author, however, had come to regard marriage and child-rearing as a 'biological trap':

> I cannot explain my pathological hatred of domestic life and frantic need to be free. Not free to write, or to be amused, or famous. To be free. To call it spiritual nausea only pushes it further out of reach. A crazily violent character, a tramp or a lunatic, shares my skin with a Yorkshire housewife.
>
> In any event, in 1915 I was, all else apart, biologically trapped.[13]

Jameson's decision to pursue a career in London after trying to make sure that her son was well cared for might have been a realistic attempt to resolve a problem that other women who are not suited to domesticity nevertheless endure.

Whereas the real-life Jameson became a successful writer and her son a competent adult, the fictional Hervey thinks that her decision to leave her son and to work in advertising in London has been a failure:

> She realized, with a dreadful clearness, that nothing she had gained for herself by coming to London compensated for what she had given up. She saw her work in the office as a mean, mind-destroying ritual, the refinement of trickery, by which she earned what just kept her alive and hired Richard a place in another woman's life. Besides that, she was not even a success at her work . . . A notion – that it was time to ask Shaw-Thomas for more money – came for the first time close, and the excitement it started brought her upright in bed.[14]

In this passage, Hervey is beginning to view the world as a man would, in that she thinks her solution to her emotional difficulty, if she cannot return to her son, is to extract more money from her employer in order to compensate her for what she has lost. Her solution is an economic and not an emotional one.

In contrast, Joan Barfoot's more recent *Gaining Ground* (1978) represents a woman cutting herself off completely from, rather than trying to accommodate herself to the late twentieth-century male-run society in which she feels that she is little more than an obliging servant. Abra silently abandons her husband, Stephen, and her two children, Elliott and Katie, and retreats to a hermit's existence on an isolated farm where she grows her own vegetables and has little contact with the outside world. Over the nine years of the novel's time-span, she gradually reorients – or disorients, depending on your point of view – herself towards the natural world. Some readers might see her flight as a middle-class dropping-out or, alternatively, as an escape from urban hell to rural paradise.

Abra's social position in the Canadian urban world had been that of a supporter of patriarchy: she married young and worked in a dress shop for four years in order that her husband, Stephen, might obtain a degree and become a stockbroker. He did this so profitably that Abra no longer needed to work. She had two children and became immersed in the role of wife and mother. But this self immolation in the service of others led to a split in her mind, so that she felt she did not belong to this family that she had helped to create. The domination of her life by male rules – that she self-sacrificially bring up her children and that she provide entertainment for her husband's colleagues – brought about her 'breakdown'.

Abra came to the conclusion that she could only save herself from complete annihilation by living on her own and by discovering herself through meditation:

> I became able, after a time, to understand that there had been what might be called a breakdown . . . Accepting the word, it became simpler. If 'breakdown' meant some terrible anguish, I had missed that part of it until now, questioning it. There had been strain, unhappiness, even fear, but nothing that could properly be called anguish. I moved to the next step: where had the breakdown come? And it came to me that all the components of the old life had, in fact, broken down: the home, the children, the marriage, whatever had made up life then. Everything else, everything outside of me, had broken down. I saw that I had not broken down. I had been put together.[15]

Because she believed her family life for her was a kind of madness, she was unable to return to her former social world when her grown-up daughter, Katie, invited her to do so.

Gaining Ground is a parable about the lives of many contemporary women which authoritarian men might do well to heed. Abra represents all those women who feel trapped in domesticity and who martyr themselves for ideals of wifehood and motherhood. These ideals suit men more than women, yet women try to keep up a social pretence of being satisfied with their martyrdom, a pretence which often results in neurotic depression. Fathers are encouraged, even though they actually live at home, to become visiting entertainers; that is, they are encouraged to do little of the nitty-gritty work of child rearing, but enjoy the pleasurable side of half-an-hour's recreation when the children are ready for bed, or make jolly visits to places of interest such as parks, zoos, museums and so on. To opt out completely and develop oneself independently of the nuclear family might be the only way some women can develop spiritually and emotionally. And, as Abra in this novel reveals, mothers are *not* indispensable:

I saw the way it was there now in that house, and the way the children were, and it stretched ahead and I could see them growing up, growing older. I could see how they would be, insecure and unsure. But they would become strong against it, testing the unsureness until they found it was untrue, and I saw that finally they might be terribly powerful, in their own ways.[16]

Perhaps 'love' itself is a fabrication in relation to mothering, a fabrication which makes women feel guilty when they think that they lack this nebulous quality. The 'love' that women experience towards their children seems to be a nurturing response that many women might have, but not all women.

To what extent has the ideal of 'mother love' been subverted in fiction through the viewpoint of a child? Joyce Reiser Kornblatt's *Nothing to Do with Love* deals with this subject ironically. The heroine, Janet Sorokin, tries to provide lovingly for her daughter, Robin, after her husband has moved out, but the child thinks that she is unloved. At the age of fifteen, she leaves home and in a children's refuge writes her account of her family:

> *One time I told my mother she made me mad because she brought work home with her every night and her face got stony; she said, 'Why is it that you don't resent your father's impossible schedule, which sometimes results in your not seeing him for weeks, while I'm here with you every day and wind up getting all the flak?' She was there every day, but not with me; and my father was gone sometimes for weeks at a time, but when I finally did spend time with him, he was there, I had all his attention, it was like I was running for president, that's how important he made me feel.*[17]

Robin has learnt that being 'loved' means being the centre of attention, and her feelings of love are those of adolescent narcissism. Yet the implication of this passage and, for that matter, the remainder of this piece of fiction, is that Janet is at fault as a mother because she has concentrated more on her work as a geneticist than on her daughter. But this story repeats the old myth: mothers should be perfect, above all else, in their relationships with their children. Perhaps the fictional answer to Robin's fictional lack of 'love' is for her to live with her father. So long as mothers think that they have to bear the brunt of the responsibility for bringing up children, then their lives, if they follow a professional career also, will be overburdened with work and the sheer grind of the daily care of minors.

In fiction about mothers and children, Joyce Cary is one of the few male authors who has penetrated the stereotypes surrounding motherhood. In one of his short stories, 'A Hot Day' (1956), for example, the narrator shows how a mother has become stuck in repetitively illogical patterns of behaviour. Her four-year-old boy is unaware of the importance of chronological time in ordered society, but he has a deep sense of timeless wonder. He has 'ten minutes' in which to have a drink before catching a bus, but, instead of drinking, he admires his straw, discovering how it blows bubbles:

> The mother mops her face and says in a resigned voice, 'There, I told you [her husband] it was all nonsense about him being thirsty.'
> 'But I *am* thirsty,' Tom says.
> 'Then why aren't you drinking?'
> Tom blows more bubbles. The bus passes; it will go to the next village, turn round and come back on the upper road. They have fifteen minutes to walk to the next stopping-place.
> The mother exclaims, 'Oh, so you're going to play with it,' and takes the glass away. Tom, subdued and guilty, says, 'May I keep the straw?'[18]

In this episode, conflict between logical commands from an authoritarian mother and non-compliant behaviour on the part of the boy is highlighted: if he is thirsty, as he claims he is, then why does he not drink quickly? But the boy responds to immediate feelings, whether they are of pleasure or discomfort. His wonder over the straw temporarily drives away his thirst, which returns when he loses interest in the straw. His mother then threatens to 'smack' him, at which he 'sits down in the road. He's in despair. What can he do if people won't believe him. He'd rather die than move another step.'[19] The mother's punitive attitude to the small boy's incomprehension of chronological time and his succumbing to each new feeling one after the other, merely drives the boy into despair which prevents his co-operating at all. If she showed any recognition of his feelings, he might then be able to move on.

In another short story, 'Babes in the Wood' (1953), however, mothers are represented as socially oppressed. But even when disaster occurs – a pram-bound baby throws, unnoticed, his mother's money out of her purse – such women are shown as still spontaneous in their maternal *jouissance*:

> The baby looked up at the two women. Its expression did not change, but as its hand flung another penny into the air, almost against its own nose, it blinked. The women cried out together.

'Ducky.'
'Little pet.'
Both were smiling in the same expression of delight; self-forgetful, innocent, foolish, fond.[20]

The women's enjoyment of the baby has not been crushed by the weight of the exploitation under which they exist:

Mothers and wives already late with their shopping, already agonised by the thought of hungry families and broken time-tables, thrust bags and prams against prams and backs. Their faces set in fierce resolution, their eyes glaring at anyone who dares even a murmur of protest, are those of soldiers in the front line who know that they fight for a good, a righteous cause; that their hearts are pure.[21]

The mothers' fortitude in the face of the demands of exhausting and unpaid labour is humorously compared to that of soldiers who at least earn their livelihood from their militaristic employment. In this story, Cary gets to grips with the dual nature of motherhood: the hard work that engenders resentment and even despair in mothers, which can be set against the emotional responses of gratification and delight.

Women novelists have paid scant attention to fictionalising the roles of mother substitutes, except for that of the stepmother. The narrator in Christina Stead's *The Man Who Loved Children* (1940) turns the stereotype of the wicked stepmother on its head, since in this novel, the stepdaughter, Louisa, murders Henrietta, her neurotic and unloving stepmother:

'. . . it is true – I got some cynanide out of your darkroom and put it in a pill-box . . . I got it out of Mother's room the night before, and I meant to put it in both cups, but I lost my nerve, I suppose; I didn't quite know what I was doing, I only put it in one cup. I got frightened.' She became sober, depressed . . .
'. . . you make up the damnedest, stupidest, most melodramatic lie I ever heard in all my born days . . . If you think I believe that cock-and-bull nonsense you made up out of your soft, addled melodramatic bean,' he [Sam, her father] said with rough good humour, 'you have another thunk coming, my girl. You are going to stay with me until you get out of this stupid adolescent crisis, and that's all there is to it.'
'Then you don't believe me?'
'Of course not.'[22]

Sam, who has self-sacrificially given his time to his children since his wife began to take drugs and neglect them, cannot face the idea that he has fathered a murderer in Louisa.

Ivy Compton-Burnett's *The Present and the Past* (1953) constructs an upper middle-class household in which the mother substitutes of nanny and governess undertake the physical labour of bringing up five children while the mother/stepmother symbolically holds on to maternal and social power. Cassius's divorced first wife, Catherine, returns to visit him and his second wife, Flavia, their two boys by his first marriage, and the three children by his second. Catherine's visit is too stressful for Cassius: he attempts suicide, recovers, but subsequently dies of a heart attack. Flavia, stepmother to Fabian and Guy, offers them a choice of home with herself or with their natural mother, Catherine, which leads to a discussion of the respective roles of both:

> 'It is a hard question,' said her stepson [Fabian], after a pause that told of obedience rather than need. 'We must be drawn in two ways. You have been the mother of our childhood, and that seems to be the greatest thing. But our childhood will pass. And only a real mother can be a mother to men. The time will get nearer and nearer. We must think of the whole of our lives.'
> 'You choose to go with your own mother?'
> 'Yes, I choose that.'[23]

Here the narrator, through Fabian, reasserts the old assumption about the natural mother being more necessary to a child than any mother substitute. Moreover, he is shown as not giving any weight to his relationships with hired servants, such as his governess.

Possibly the construction of Mrs Ramsay in Virginia Woolf's *To the Lighthouse* (1927) is one of the most detailed portraits in fiction this century of a mother's partly self-inflicted martyrdom. This novel opens with a familial triptych of mother, father and son. Mrs Ramsay has just told her son, James, that the weather will be fine enough for them to make a boat trip to the nearby lighthouse:

> 'But,' said his father, stopping in front of the drawing-room window, 'it won't be fine.'
> Had there been an axe handy, a poker, or any weapon that would have gashed a hole in his father's breast and killed him, there and then, James would have seized it. Such were the extremes of emotion that Mr Ramsay excited in his children's breasts by his mere presence; standing,

as now, lean as a knife, narrow as the blade of one, grinning sarcastically, not only with the pleasure of disillusioning his son and casting ridicule on his wife, who was ten thousand times better in every way than he was (James thought), but also with some secret conceit at his own accuracy of judgement.[24]

Beneath the surface of these family relationships lies hatred for the authoritarian behaviour of Mr Ramsay. Mrs Ramsay represents the commonly-held ideal of motherhood, balancing her children's needs against her husband's in a self-sacrificial manner which excludes an independent life for herself:

> . . . she did not like, even for a second, to feel finer than her husband; and further, could not bear not being entirely sure, when she spoke to him, of the truth of what she said . . . it was their relation, and his coming to her like that, openly so that anyone could see, that discomposed her . . . [25]

The fact that he is dependent on her morally and emotionally is not even to be acknowledged, since this would suppose a weakness in the 'patriarch' of the family. Although the narrator indicates the absurdity of this self-effacement by showing the ridiculousness of Mr Ramsay, she nevertheless suggests no alternative for Mrs Ramsay except that of self-sacrifice.

Mrs Ramsay's encouragement of her husband is outdone by her maternal dreams about the talents of her children:

> When she read just now to James, 'and there were numbers of soldiers with kettle-drums and trumpets', and his eyes darkened, she thought why should they grow up, and lose all that? He was the most gifted, the most sensitive of her children. But all, she thought, were full of promise. Prue, a perfect angel with the others, and sometimes now, at night especially, she took one's breath away with her beauty. Andrew – even her husband admitted that his gift for mathematics was extraordinary. And Nancy and Roger, they were both wild creatures now, scampering about over the country all day long. As for Rose, her mouth was too big, but she had a wonderful gift with her hands . . . [Mrs Ramsay] would have liked always to have had a baby. She was happiest carrying one in her arms.[26]

Here Mrs Ramsay gives the game away in that she reveals that she enjoys most having babies who are dependent on her for everything. She is the fictional opposite to Edna Pontellier and Kate

Clephane, neither of whom could bear such dependency. Mrs Ramsay also mourns here the loss of empathy with her children as they grow into adults.

Her possessive motherliness is ended by her death at the age of fifty. Andrew, the mathematician, is killed in the trenches during the First World War, and Prue, the beauty, dies in childbirth. Mrs Ramsay is remembered after her death, but her mothering is shown as not being indispensable to the family. Mr Ramsay takes over as sole parent, and finally James earns his grudging praise. Mrs Ramsay makes her mark, not through her children, but through becoming the central figure in Lily Briscoe's painting. What the narrator conveys is not a celebration of motherhood, but a deconstruction of the notion that striving after perfection in motherhood is necessary for the happiness of children.

May Sinclair in *Life and Death of Harriett Frean* (1922) shows a converse side to supposedly 'good' mothering by representing parents who combine to affect adversely their daughter's sexual responses. Through the juxtaposition of fragmentary episodes in Harriett's life, the narrator presents the growth and development of the heroine's psyche from babyhood to old age:

> Her mother said . . . [the nursery rhyme, 'Pussycat, pussycat, where have you been?'] three times. And each time Baby Harriett laughed. The sound of her laugh was so funny that she laughed again at that; she kept on laughing, with shriller and shriller squeals.[27]

The symbolism in this incident indicates perhaps a perverse sexuality, since in their bedtime game Harriett's father is the 'Pussycat' and Harriett is 'the little mouse in her hole under the bedclothes'. But the narrator is not explicit, and the reader must interpret Harriett's behaviour for herself, in the same way as she might try to understand an actual baby who has not yet attained speech.

The narrator also implies rather than specifies the manner in which Harriett is manipulated so that she learns to behave in the way her parents suggest. In the following episode, Harriett's mother has insisted that she lend her favourite doll, Ida, to her friend, Connie. Harriett's response is narrated in free indirect discourse coupled with direct story-telling and a piece of internal monologue:

If only she could have told Mamma what it felt like to see Connie with Ida in her arms, squeezing her tight to her chest and patting her as if Ida had been *her* child. She kept on saying to herself that Mamma didn't know; she didn't know what she had done. And when it was all over she took the wax doll and put her in the long narrow box she had come in, and buried her in the bottom drawer in the spare room wardrobe. She thought, 'If I can't have her to myself I won't have her at all. I've got Emily. I shall just have to pretend she's not an idiot.'

She pretended Ida was dead; lying in her pasteboard coffin and buried in the wardrobe cemetery.[28]

The description of this incident presages Harriett's fate: she herself is treated as an object by her over-possessive parents and lives in a metaphorical coffin of repressed desires.

Harriett is encouraged to suppress any experience which appears 'ugly', especially anything related to perverse sexuality. Although she is allowed to read the latest theories (this novel is set in the latter half of the nineteenth century) of Darwin, Huxley and Herbert Spencer, the behaviour of a sexual pervert whom she encounters in Black's Lane is never explained to her by her parents:

> But three years went before Harriett understood how wise they had been, and why her mother took her again and again to Black's Lane to pick red campion, so that it was always the red campion she remembered. They must have known all the time about Black's Lane; Annie, the housemaid, used to say it was a bad place; something had happened to a little girl there . . . Then one day, when she was thirteen, standing by the apple tree, Connie Hancock told her. A secret . . . Behind the dirty blue palings . . . She shut her eyes, squeezing the lids down, frightened. But when she thought of the lane she could see nothing but the green banks, the three tall elms, and the red campion pushing through the white froth of the cow parsley . . .[29]

Harriett's upbringing leaves her stunted sexually, unable to feel anything except a desire to behave well according to her parents' standards. She suppresses her desire for her friend's fiancé, Robin and, later, rejects the sight of her servant, Maggie, breast-feeding her illegitimate baby. Harriett comes to depend on Maggie as if she herself were Maggie's baby. She dies in her sixties of a cancerous tumour, which in her fantasy becomes a dead baby. The narrator thus relates Harriett's experience of obsessive mothering to her fantasies at the moment of death in which Harriett imagines that her friend, Connie, is her long-dead mother.

Perhaps these fictional mothers, except Edna Pontellier in Chopin's *The Awakening*, have been constructed by their authors in the light of what Judith Barrington terms the 'patriarchal voice':

> *Mothers are selfless; you have no right to expect the children to go away when you need to work; they are always the priority; it is heartless to resent their existence; you should always meet their needs; they will be terribly damaged if you cannot give them unconditional love; how can you possibly expect them to understand your needs; you are not supposed to have needs; you are an adult, they are children; mothers never act selfishly; it is selfish to want to do anything without them; put their needs first; always be available . . .*[30]

Virginia Woolf's Mrs Ramsay could be said to epitomise in fiction this imaginary 'selfless' mother, although even she is shown by the narrator to be not indispensable if the second parent is allowed to become competent. And Stead's flawed, neurotic, drug-taking mother, Henrietta, in *The Man Who Loved Children* has failed mainly in terms of what a patriarchal society expects of stepmothers or, for that matter, mothers. Judith Barrington, who writes about being persecuted by an inner patriarchal 'voice', is herself a non-biological mother who has taken on the role of co-parent to the adopted mixed-race children of her lesbian lover. This unusual real-life set-up prompts the question of how the subject of the non-nuclear family has been treated, if at all, in twentieth-century fiction.

5

Alternatives to marriage

To what extent have our women novelists written about any alternatives to the pursuit of the heterosexual 'marital bliss' that is so often at the heart of some fiction? Do women find more freedom by taking lovers, living in communes, or making homes with their own sex? In recent twentieth-century fiction, some women are represented as wanting to cut themselves off completely from the dominance of men, especially from that male craving for power which is often evident in sexual relationships. Celibacy and lesbianism, are, for some women, the only responses to the problem of how to free themselves from male power.

Celibacy is a prominent theme in May Sarton's *The Magnificent Spinster* (1985), in which the life story of Jane Reid, a schoolteacher, is narrated by seventy-year-old Cam, one of her former pupils who became a lesbian historian. In an attempt at verisimilitude, Cam is represented by the 'concealed' narrator – the person actually telling the story of Cam's telling the story – as an amateur novelist who mixes supposed 'facts', such as letters, with material that she has ostensibly imagined about this supposedly living person. Whenever Cam has a 'block' or a dry period she looks up people who knew Jane Reid. Thus readers are given much supposedly unedited material about Jane and we must try ourselves to answer questions already raised about, for example, the nature of Jane's sexual orientation and experience. Since the information about Jane is usually only partial, because Cam's informants supposedly do not know any more, readers never understand enigmatic Jane. This seeming verisimilitude mirrors life in that we can only guess at other people's life stories because of incomplete information.

Cam, the narrator within the narration, makes up the early events of Jane's life before the First World War, in order to answer one of the significant questions of this novel: why did Jane never experience sexuality of a hetero- or homosexual kind? Was it because her sexuality had been queered in early youth by her parents, who allowed her, as a young teenager, to go to the theatre with a young man, Maurice, but, as soon as she became old enough to offend propriety by being unchaperoned, abruptly cut off this relationship? After fabricating what is essentially a romantic story, Cam cuts in with a piece of psychoanalytic theorising mixed with supposed 'facts':

> I have chosen to dwell on Maurice and that friendship at some length because, as I think over Jane's life, it seems clear to me that it was of great importance in her growth as a human being, and perhaps the enforced parting set her on a course she would follow to the end of her life . . .
>   It is odd that, on the whole, novelists speak little of friendship between opposite sexes, and especially these days, when sexual encounters dominate everything else in most fictional characters. I am writing about a woman who had a genius for friendship with both sexes, and touched deeply an enormous number and variety of lives. Could she have done so to the same extent, and at the same depth, had she married? I think not. It is one of the questions I hope to be able to probe as I pursue my quarry.[1]

Through her narrator, Cam, the concealed narrator has convincingly made up what Jane's early life might have been but, instead of continuing in this vein, Cam proceeds to deconstruct the form of semi-biographical fiction, revealing gaps in her knowledge of what happened to Jane, and suggesting that she might not be able to make up any more satisfactory fiction about her. This technical device of 'story within a story' might have been intended to induce credibility. The fun for readers is to produce our own text from the scanty information that Cam, with her arbitrary research methods, is able to discover.

Despite this innovative and somewhat promising beginning, it is an uphill job for the reader to fill in for the narrator and produce a text which gives a coherent understanding of Jane's life. Much of what follows from the narrator is platitudinous, such as the following passage in which Cam asks why Jane did not marry her one serious suitor, Sam Dawson:

What did she know or guess about herself that informed her decision? Partly perhaps that she was attracted to Sam, but not passionately attracted, partly that marriage would mean giving up her freedom – every woman, especially these days, recognizes this and has to come to terms with it. For the rest of her life, Jane, as I observed her, entered into families as a kind of fairy godmother whisking an exhausted mother away for a weekend, inviting a whole family of seven children and their parents to the island for a week, so that the mother could have a real rest. Possibly she sensed that her way of being a mother would turn out to be mothering the mothers.[2]

But how does a woman 'come to terms with' her loss of freedom at marriage? Traditionally, women who marry are seen as gaining a new freedom, such as enjoying sexuality unfettered by moral restrictions. On the other hand, since the era of 1960s 'permissiveness', some women might now find such freedom illusory. Moreover, this summary of Jane's fairy godmothering is more the stuff of social work than of dramatic interest.

Celibacy as an attribute of heroines in twentieth-century novels is rare, but lesbianism in novels is becoming less so. Joanna Russ's *On Strike Against God* (1980) sets out to shock the male hegemony in the academic and heterosexual world with the pleasures of lesbian love-making. But perhaps male readers, even if they fear lesbianism, will find this novel sexually titillating. The most striking aspect of this novel, however, is not the lesbianism in defiance of patriarchy – the 'strike' against God, the father – but the subtle delineation of male selfishness and dominance in the academic world. The heroine, Esther, is an academic in literary studies who is the sexual prey of male colleagues:

He told me the names of his last four articles, which had been published in various places; he told me where, and then he told me what the editors had said about them (the articles) . . . So I analyzed the strengths of all those separate editors and journals and praised all of them; I said I admired him and it was really something to get into those journals, as I very well knew.

'I often wonder why women have careers,' said Shredded Napkin [her mental nickname for him] suddenly, showing his teeth . . .

'At least you're still – uh – decorative!' he said, winking . . .

I said quickly, 'Oh my, I've got to go,' and he looked disappointed. He's beginning to like me. I am a better and better audience as I get numbed, and although I've played this game of Impress You before (and won it, too – though I don't like either of the prizes; winning is too much like losing) I'm too tired to go on playing tonight. Will he insist on taking me home? Will he ask me out? Will he fight over the bill? Will he start making remarks about women being this or that, or tell me I'm a good woman because I'm not competitive?[3]

This satire of a male academic building up his ego while denigrating the aspirations of women academics – suggesting that being 'decorative' is as important as one's career, for example – succeeds because this fictional version, as female academics and students know from experience, is related to what happens in the actual world.

The satiric thrust of this novel peters out when Esther 'falls in love' with a woman and a lesbian paradise is evoked in language which is banal:

She lay mistrustfully on her stomach and I knelt between her legs, gaily pounding away at her shoulder-blades . . . I . . . slid down to the rose between her legs. That's exactly what it is. Amazing. (Medieval stories.)
. . .
Blushing very deeply, she asked me if she could do something. I said yes, of course. She averted her face and moved my hand on to her rose (sorry to be so kvetchily sentimental).[4]

From this description, the reader is left bemused about whether the first-person narrator is referring, in her use of the metaphor, 'rose', to the anus or clitoris, or perhaps both. Moreover the rose as a symbol in love poetry comes with medieval chivalric overtones and strikes not so much an anachronistic as a bathetic note in this late twentieth-century radical satire that aspires to be revelatory to heterosexual women.

One of the difficulties for feminists is that of accommodating themselves within a patriarchal society and, at the same time, subverting it. In the above fiction, the inevitable confrontation between dominating male and subversive female seems to have been shunted off into a lesbian alternative. But in Marge Piercy's *The High Cost of Living* (1978), the bisexual heroine, Leslie, sticks with the hegemony of male sociology in order to further her own career. Leslie is nevertheless portrayed as being well aware of the habits of the macho male in the form of another research assistant, Mark Hennessy:

She tried waiting him out, but he waited too. Could he really think not wearing a bra was an automatic general come-on? . . . He was inching his chin forward again until he had walked it well into the space she counted as her own, forcing her against the mis-shapen back of the chair. She imagined lashing out with her foot, a quick chop to topple him. Her mouth twitched in a quarter smile.

Taking that for encouragement, he reached for her hand. Big hot grasp. She could not kick him, because they worked together for George: Professor Sanderson. George was her bread and butter, her thesis adviser, almost her fate. George had brought her along to Detroit and the University when he had changed jobs, carried her along with an appointment as his research assistant with his files and his map collection. Therefore, she could not kick the chair out from under Hennessy, but she could pull her hand away. 'Sorry. I have to pee.'[5]

Leslie takes evasive action from a man here, despite her friendship with her boss. This heterosexual professor accepts her lesbianism, but his almost voyeuristic curiosity about her sexual relationships suggests that he takes both less and more than a professional sociological interest in her behaviour. When his neighbours tell him that Leslie as a caretaker used his house to entertain her 'gay' male friend, he comments, 'That's a new one. Those in the straight world who used to ponder what lesbians do together can put that in the hopper and bounce it around'.[6] Which suggests that he himself will 'bounce it around' in his own 'hopper' of fantasies.

Leslie has an equivocal position in that she espouses feminism and yet she is assisting in patriarchal sociological studies. This paradox is dramatised in the form of a discussion between Leslie and her feminist friends:

'But writing came in around the beginning of patriarchy,' Sherry said. She smiled a lot as she argued, as if to make contact across the words. 'The first thing they did with it was to cover up the past. To rewrite the old myths. How can you expect we'll ever find a nice box in the desert with a scroll in it saying, "This is how things were before the male revolution, folks," with nice cross-dating in a language you happen to be able to read.'

'But your history isn't history, it's comic books. You just make it up wholesale to be the way you want it to be,' Leslie said coldly . . . Tasha was saying, 'You still admire that macher George. You think his way is *the* way. What are these damn Simpson papers you talk about? They're just a bunch of rich crooks. Essentially they're paying you off to put their house in order.'

'But they had an effect on how things are here. They made choices that shaped Detroit.'. . .

'Leslie, why don't you get involved in the women's school? Use your skill now for us . . . You could do a history course. Local. Women's history. Whatever.'

'Not old wives' tales, which is all you people care about,' Leslie said gruffly. 'I don't have the time.'[7]

In the character of Leslie, embryo sociologist, is epitomised the dichotomy women feminists currently experience between recognition of the importance of intuitive feeling and imagination as set against logical and factual explanations of phenomena. Women's studies means the study of anything to do with women. Such 'studies' tend to be ghettoised because some critics think that an inherent weakness exists in the 'feminine' and that, moreover, women's thinking is bound to lack form and order because of woman's intrinsically inchoate nature. In a reverse prejudice, some women try to avoid any systematising of knowledge because for them system smacks of the authoritarianism of a social order that they regard as 'patriarchal'. Nevertheless, even French feminists, who tend to be more *avant-garde* than their British or American counterparts, acknowledge the need for feminist logicians and rhetoricians.

Hélène Cixous and Catherine Clément, in *The Newly Born Woman*, demonstrate in the following dialogue the necessity for using both kinds of voices – the rhetoric of logical categorising and the poetry of free-flowing intuition and fantasy:

C[atherine]: Yours is a writing halfway between theory and fiction. Whereas my discourse is, or tries to be, more demonstrative and discursive, following the most traditional method of rhetorical demonstration . . .

H[élène]: I distrust the identification of a subject with a single discourse. First, there is the discourse that suits the occasion. I use rhetorical discourse, the discourse of mastery, orally, for example, with my students, and obviously I do it on purpose; it is a refusal on my part to leave organized discourse entirely in men's power . . . There will not be *one* feminine discourse, there will be thousands of different kinds of feminine words, and then there will be the code for general communication, philosophical discourse, rhetoric like now but with a great number of subversive discourses in addition . . .[8]

The characterisation of Leslie might be read as a fictional representation of the split between patriarchal logic and feminine intuition, and her approach might suggest a way in which a *rapprochement* between the two ways of thinking could be found.

Also, Piercy's *The High Cost of Living* centres on the idealistic fanaticism of lesbian feminists who ape heterosexual pairing behaviour even when they live in communes. In regard to theories of feminism, the narrator implies mockery of their artsy-craftsy courses which lead nowhere, suggesting subversively that women's studies are not good *per se*. The narrator's parodying, through the voice of Leslie, of inept methods of feminist historical analysis can be extrapolated to apply to some feminist literary critics who think that merely to list their favourite (or, indeed, unfavourite) women authors is an adequate method of researching women's fiction. Nicola Beauman, for example, in *A Very Great Profession* (1983), leaves out, in this survey of twentieth-century women writers, substantial women authors such as Jean Rhys and Ivy Compton-Burnett. The concept of an enabling 'sisterhood' might be supportive, but nevertheless maturity can only come about through the writings of our 'sisters' being subjected to similar standards of appraisal to those used in 'patriarchal' writing and research.

In fiction which openly explores the possibilities for women of living together in couples or groups of women only, these female alliances are usually peripheral to the main plot. In *The High Cost of Living*, Leslie visits her former lover, Val, only to find that she feels rejected because she is not part of a couple. According to the narrator of these fictional events, solitary women such as Leslie are alienated as much from homosexual couples as from heterosexual ones. Leslie observes that to live in a women's community necessitates forming a love relationship with another woman in order to be accepted:

> Another couple dropped in, Vicki and Meg. Like Liz and Mary they had children, they rented an old farmhouse, although they raised only a few vegetables, they lived on marginal jobs and little money. Joints traveled around the table, they drank the coarse wine and gossiped. She [Leslie] tried to stir herself and ask about everything she should be interested in . . . She felt cut off from the women in the room. If she were living here alone, having lost her lover, they would be wary of her. She had seen it ten times. Couples. She would be lonely here without Valerie, she would be forced to find another lover just to be welcomed back into the community again. This was the only place she had ever found acceptance as a lesbian, yet the narrowness of the world they created here grated upon her for the first time.[9]

Leslie prefers to try to make it in the patriarchal academic world independently of women's groups, and to make relationships with individuals she meets, rather than group relationships with these small-time farmer women or the proponents of women's studies who want her to teach 'women's history'. Nevertheless, she serves women by teaching them karate – which she learned from a male instructor – for purposes of self-defence. The fictional world of *The High Cost of Living* generally is a mixture of heterosexual and homosexual relationships which are equally subject to narcissism and self-seeking.

Another novel in which communal living arrangements and/or homosexual relationships between women are peripheral to the main plot is Grace Bartram's *Peeling*. Ally, the central character, who is abandoned by her husband, turns to voluntary work in a women's refuge from wife-beaters. She discovers her sympathy for these women who are not lesbians though they exist on the fringe of society, barely acknowledged by the state. They are also an implied threat to patriarchy in that they are a reminder of the disorders inherent in the violent misuse of male power. Ally's ex-husband, Rowley, who tends to be a stereotype of the egocentric deserting male, also echoes male stereotypes about the nature of women's refuges:

> 'Do you have any idea what kind of reputation that place has got, Ally? Women who go there are called sluts. I had some of them pointed out to me and I don't understand you mixing with women like that.'. . .
> 'It isn't really like you think or like you've heard around the town. That's male prejudice, hurt pride. Men seem to think it's a slur on them, personally, that there's a need for women's refuges.'[10]

In real life, although the concept of women's refuges might not seem a personal 'slur' to each individual male, the necessity for them is an implied criticism of the institution of marriage in which men still tend to abrogate authoritarian rights to themselves, even if 'obey' is deleted from the marriage service. In *Peeling*, Ally works in a women's refuge in order to restore her self-esteem after her marriage has broken up. Even when she is acknowledging self-insight which she has acquired from one of the working-class women whom she has befriended in the refuge, her gratitude is tinged with patronage:

Winnie came in with two mugs of coffee and settled herself on the floor
at Ally's feet.
'Winnie, when you get depressed, what do you do?'
'What do you mean, what do I do?'
'I mean . . . what do you do about the feeling? Does it frighten you?
Are you scared you won't come out of it?'
'No! I always come out of it . . . It's a fuckin' nuisance, getting attacks
of being depressed, but I know I'll come out of it. I always do. Everyone
does, don't they?'. . .
'You mean, you're kind of patient about it?'
'Yes, I had to learn that. I mean, if you don't, you're dead, aren't you?'
Winnie grinned. 'Hey, I'm counselling you, aren't I?'
'You sure are, Winnie. Thank you. That sorted something out for me.'
She smiled at the woman . . . They were all in it together, everyone
had problems of one kind or another.[11]

But Ally has not confided in Winnie the source of her depression,
nor her experience of despair when her husband left her. She lets
Winnie get coffee for her and sit at her feet, and when Winnie has
indirectly explained how to work through depression by submitting
to its pain, Ally thinks of her impersonally as 'the woman', who,
despite her kindness, is seen as inferior to middle-class Ally. The
narrator has a blind spot about how Ally has bludged her way
through life, living off Rowley even after her daughter, Jane, left
home. At the conclusion of the novel, although Ally understand-
ably refuses to be reconciled with Rowley, she nevertheless allows
herself to continue to be supported economically by him.

The central ideas in this novel are not feminist, since Ally is not
shown as questioning why she has never supported herself after her
marriage. The description of the 'women's refuge' seems merely a
device for representing one more bourgeois middle-class woman's
individual growth at the cost of an exploration of the nature of
women's economic and political position.

In contrast, Elizabeth Jolley's various novels are often quirky
exposés of communal life, sometimes specifically that of women.
But Jolley's communities are those that have come about through a
shared occupation rather than a response to the human need for
companionship. In *Miss Peabody's Inheritance* (1983), the girls'
boarding-school, Pine Heights, is the literary creation of the
novelist, Diana Hopewell, and the literal creation of the fictional
headmistress, Miss Thorne, who is central to the story-within-a-
story, but not central to the novel itself. The anti-heroine of this

novel is Miss Peabody, to whom Diana Hopewell addresses her novel in the form of letters from Australia (where Hopewell lives) to England (the home of Miss Peabody). Miss Peabody is a spinster who lives with her demanding mother. But, through her epistolary exchange with Diana Hopewell, Miss Peabody begins to take life at least by the fingertips at the office where she works as a typist.

The narrator urges us to notice the effects of vicarious novel-reading on our own lives, as well as commenting on how the family is not the only way of enjoying companionship. Miss Thorne and her assistant, Miss Edgely, for example, have an emotional as well as a business relationship. Miss Thorne dominates, partly because of her position as Miss Edgely's employer, and partly because of her ruthless methods of meeting her own sexual needs. In the following episode, which is characteristic of Miss Thorne's methods of seduction of a willing victim, they are caught out by one of their pupils, Gwenda, whom they have taken abroad to Europe because Miss Thorne is attracted to her. She has spent a night in Gwenda's bed, which collapsed beneath them. Gwenda has quickly abandoned Miss Thorne because she intends to marry Mr Frome, the widowed father of one of her schoolfriends. Miss Thorne has to fall back on Miss Edgely who has been feeling excluded:

> The night is warm, Miss Thorne pours a substantial brandy for Miss Edgely and lines up a little fortification of double whiskies, in prudent containers, on the bedside table.
> 'Come away to bed swee-sweedle,' Miss Thorne decides it is too warm a night for nightdresses . . .
> 'Come in!' Miss Thorne, half asleep, raises her head as she hears the little knock on the door. 'Come in!' she calls before she is fully awake. She hears Gwenda's soft voice.
> 'I'm back Miss Thorne.'
> Miss Thorne, trying to pull the counterpane quickly over her own and Miss Edgely's sleeping nakedness, sees the startled look on the girl's face as she draws back immediately from the remarkable scene.
> 'Good night Miss Thorne.' The door closes quickly with a firm little click. Miss Thorne hears this final click with more pain than relief . . .
> Perhaps the gel [Gwenda] could understand, she thinks to herself, perhaps the gel could understand something of the real need people have in themselves, a need matching needs in other people.[12]

The narrator, through the fictional novelist, Diana Hopewell, insists here that the human need for affection – which is partly lust –

is common to young and old, whether heterosexually- or homosexually-oriented. And sexual orientation itself is shown to be partly a response to chance, since if Gwenda had not met and been proposed to by Mr Frome, who also sought to meet his own need for 'love', she would have remained locked in her crush on Miss Thorne.

And Miss Thorne, through her narrator, Diana Hopewell, makes a telling comment on the advantages of the single life as compared to the disadvantages of married love and procreation:

> Without wanting them to, thoughts of school came into her mind. The three friends, the three junior mistresses . . . all of them so eager, and in their individual ways, good little mothers . . . She thinks too about the three young women, how, not so very long ago all of them must have been pleased, excited, delighted to be loved and chosen to be married. And all three have, more than once, for love and other mysterious reasons, gone through the bearing of their children. In the first place the months of carrying the child and then the giving birth to the child, and, even more arduous perhaps, the task of caring and feeding and other additional burdens attached in general to the bringing up of children. It is not the first time that Miss Thorne has been confronted by this apparent paradox of human behaviour. And here she was stout and well fed, able to travel twice a year as a rule, as cheaply as possible of course but comfortably; here she was lying in bed contemplating the terminating of their employment. Perhaps ending, if only temporarily, their livelihood.[13]

The narrator, through Hopewell's creation, Miss Thorne, shows how lesbians ironically have the pleasures of love and companionship without the ordeal of giving birth to and bringing up children. Through comic satire, the narrator takes a steel-spiked thrust at the ideal of heterosexual love and marrige.

May Sarton in *A Reckoning* (1978) also challenges received notions about the fulfilling nature of heterosexual love and the procreation and nurture of children. In this novel, Laura Spelman, who is dying of cancer, is represented as recollecting the most important people in her life. In her self-examination, Laura recognises that her husband, Charles, has not responded to her with the depth of emotion she believed she required:

> In the last few years Charles had been the only person with whom she shared her life on the deepest level, and – equally important – on the most

trivial; but because he was a man there were areas of her being that she could not share with him. He was not good about discussing feelings, for instance.[14]

But his inability to discuss 'feelings' might not be because he is masculine. The narrator is expressing a stereotyped opinion about men which tends to compromise the truth of Laura's discovery that she prefers a woman friend, Ella, to her husband.

By the conclusion of the novel, the dying Laura is shown as believing that only Ella, and their early non-physical friendship, were important to her:

'One thing about this journey [of recollection] has been an entirely new understanding about what women can mean for one another, and men for one another . . . We [she and Ella] were very different, and yet whenever we met it was as though we became one person in two bodies . . . there was a kind of understanding, of shared response to everything from art to landscapes, to food, to people. Being with her I became fully myself.[15]

This memory of Laura's 'love' for Ella has echoes of *Mrs Dalloway*, in that Clarissa Dalloway at fifty recalls her early infatuation for Sally Seton, with an implication that she had been more stimulated by Sally than by her husband, Richard Dalloway, or by another man who courted her, Peter Walsh:

But this question of love (she thought, putting her coat away), this falling in love with women. Take Sally Seton; her relation in the old days with Sally Seton. Had not that, after all, been love? . . . they all went out onto the terrace and walked up and down . . . She and Sally fell a little behind. Then came the most exquisite moment of her whole life, passing a stone urn with flowers in it. Sally stopped; picked a flower; kissed her on the lips. The whole world might have turned upside down! The others disappeared; there she was alone with Sally. And she felt that she had been given a present, wrapped up, and told just to keep it, not to look at it – a diamond, something infinitely precious, wrapped up, which, as they walked (up and down, up and down), she uncovered, or the radiance burnt through, the revelation, the religious feeling![16]

Clarissa is never shown experiencing this kind of excitement with a man, although she thinks that she might have had 'gaiety' had she married Peter Walsh: 'It was all over for her. The sheet was stretched and the bed narrow.'[17] Although Clarissa Dalloway had one child, Elizabeth, by her marriage, she feels sexually unfulfilled.

The concealed narrator in *Mrs Dalloway* moves from one constructed consciousness to another, so that the reader cannot make definitive statements about whether any of the 'loves' imputed to Clarissa Dalloway are important to her. But the concealed narrator in *A Reckoning* expresses implicit propaganda about the supposed overriding need for tenderness between women:

> Finally she [Laura on her deathbed] managed to say, 'Communion. Something women are only beginning to tap, to understand, a kind of tenderness towards each other as women . . . Strange that we were not lovers. Why not?'
> 'My God, Laura, surely you remember the atmosphere of scandal, worse, of sin, around any such relationship at that time! We had been poisoned by the whole ethos, taught to be mortally afraid of what our bodies tried to teach us. Besides we were the marrying kind. A passionate love would have created terrible conflict.'[18]

The notion of 'sisterhood' that is represented in this passage might be one means of establishing better relationships between women. But Laura's belief in an idealised love between women overlooks the power relationships and exploitation which can exist between women and women as well as between women and men.

Women's fiction of the 1980s about women's 'love' relationships with women tends to present such women in couples which are similar to heterosexual couples in both ideals and behaviour. What is common to idealised dreams about both heterosexual and homosexual relationships is a romantic belief that each person might find another – a 'right' person – with whom he or she can engage in sexual relations. Thus, in Nicky Edwards's *Mud*, which is partly a novel about the contemporary women's scene, and partly about the First World War, the language used by the first-person narrator, Jo, and her putative lover, Beryl, could be exchanged for that of a heterosexual couple:

> 'What do you want?'
> 'Are you asking me my intentions?'
> 'Um.' I havered. 'Possibly.'
> 'Well, I don't know that I have any as such . . . maybe this is all a bit daft and over-formal, and too much like an everyday story of right-on folk trying to decide if they're compatible.' She took a deep breath and put on a self-protecting 'you don't have to take this seriously' voice. 'But I don't just want you for your body, you know.'[19]

Romantic clichés such as 'asking me my intentions' and 'I don't just want you for your body' have already been debased in romantic fiction about heterosexual 'love' relationships. In this novel, the relationship between Jo, the young embryo writer, and Ada, the eighty-seven-year-old whom she is interviewing in order to construct a drama about the First World War, is more original.

Part of Alice Walker's *The Color Purple* is a first-person narrative by the protagonist, Celie, whose lesbian amours with the singer, Shug Avery, are represented in metaphors which are striking. Celie, who is projected as living in the Deep South before the Second World War, is raped at the age of fourteen by her stepfather and has two children by him, thus becoming frigid as well as sterile. Her passion for Shug Avery, who stimulates her both emotionally and sexually, is credible in the light of the girl's violent introduction to sexuality when she was an adolescent. Moreover, Shug is the former lover of the man Celie has been compelled by her father to marry, so that Celie is also paying out her husband whom she does not love, and who still has a passion for Shug Avery. And because Celie's first-person voice in her 'letters to God' is constructed in an appropriate dialect, the reader responds with interest to her account of her first experience of sexual pleasure:

> My mama die, I tell Shug. My sister Nettie run away. Mr — come git me to take care his rotten children. He never ast me nothing bout myself. He clam on top of me and fuck and fuck, even when my head bandaged. Nobody ever love me, I say.
>
> She say, I love you, Miss Celie. And then she haul off and kiss me on the mouth.
>
> *Um*, she say, like she surprise. I kiss her back, say, *um*, too. Us kiss and kiss till us can't hardly kiss no more. Then us touch each other.
>
> I don't know nothing bout it, I say to Shug.
>
> I don't know much, she say.
>
> Then I feels something real soft and wet on my breast, feel like one of my little lost babies mouth.
>
> Way after while, I act like a little lost baby too . . . Me and Shug sound asleep. Her back to me, my arms round her waist. What it like? Little like sleeping with mama, only I can't hardly remember ever sleeping with her. Little like sleeping with Nettie only sleeping with Nettie never feel this good. It warm and cushiony, and I feel Shug's big tits sorta flop over my arms like suds. It feel like heaven is what it feel like, not like sleeping with Mr — at all.[20]

This representation of Celie describing her sexual behaviour with

Shug seems authentic in its comparison of the experience with mothering and being mothered. Celie's similes are in keeping with her past experiences. Her mode of expression is constructed to fit her character, whereas very often in women's fiction the speech of the characters seems to emerge directly from the bourgeois author's own life or to emanate from women's studies' textbooks; for example, the first-person narrator in Nicky Edwards's *Mud* uses feminist jargon such as 'personal space' and 'reclaiming her own life'.[21]

In order to hold the reader's interest, fiction of the traditional kind depends upon conflict, whether the conflict arises between characters or between character and event. Innovative fiction which does away with character construction and plot development has so far mainly been the option taken by French feminist authors, such as Simone de Beauvoir. Realistic fiction about love between women, such as May Sarton's *A Reckoning*, tends to show women without conflict in a happy *rapprochement* which resembles nothing so much as pulp fiction about anodyne heterosexual love relationships. Moreover, women's fiction, even when themes such as politics and war are central, tends always to include sexual relationships whether homo- or heterosexual.

Where is our late twentieth-century female Conrad? This early twentieth-century novelist used his seafaring experience to write fiction about, among other things, maturity and death. Despite the fact that in Conrad's fiction such as *The Shadow-Line* and *The Secret Sharer* the cast is entirely male, a reader of either sex can respond to the narrator's comments about the meaning of human experience. No women writers, apart from a few who have constructed subversive Utopias in their science fiction, have attempted to portray an all-female working world in which sexual relationships – whether of the homo- or heterosexual kind – play little or no part.

6

Politics and war

'The personal is political.' By adopting this slogan, which originated in the 'permissive' 1960s, women have turned their own interest in the personal to their advantage. In theories about 'sexual politics', the personal sexual relationship is shown to hold overtones of domination and submission, with generally the male dominating the female. Kate Millett claims that, until the balance of power shifts, especially in sexual relationships, to equality between the sexes, no change in systematised male supremacy will occur:

> unless the ideology of real or fantasized virility is abandoned, unless the clinging to male supremacy as a birthright is finally foregone, all systems of oppression will continue to function simply by virtue of their logical and emotional mandate in the primary human situation.[1]

According to Millett, this sexual domination by men over women is taken for granted, not only in the bedroom, but in every sphere:

> What goes largely unexamined, often even unacknowledged (yet is institutionalized nonetheless) in our social order is the birthright priority whereby males rule females. Through this system a most ingenious form of 'interior colonization' has been achieved. It is one which tends moreover to be sturdier than any form of segregation, and more rigorous than class stratification, more uniform, certainly more enduring. However muted its present appearance may be, sexual dominion obtains nevertheless as perhaps the most pervasive ideology of our culture and provides its most fundamental concept of power . . .[2]

Millett applies her social theorising to a literary deconstruction of a few male authors, in which she asserts that only Jean Genet, the French dramatist, has 'transcended the sexual myths of our era'; for example, in *The Balcony*, he 'explores the pathology of virility, the chimera of sexual congress as a paradigm of power over other human beings'.[3] Since Kate Millett's criticism of authors such as Norman Mailer, Henry Miller and D. H. Lawrence appeared, women writers have become more aware of patriarchal and sexist ideologies which are expressed in both male and female fiction.

If fiction is either imbued with or subverts the cultural world-views of its period, then what of twentieth-century fiction by women in relation to male power in all spheres? Are there many female authors who attempt in their work to overturn the patriarchal customs and rules which are linked to sexual power and virility? Only a few women writers in the first half of the twentieth century have engaged with the problems of the inequalities of women *vis-à-vis* men.

Twentieth-century women's novels can be roughly divided into two periods, that is, pre- and post-1960. Prior to 1960, we can discover novels which can be said to trace or present the ideas and beliefs of 'first wave feminism', that is, the movement during the early part of this century towards achieving equality for women, especially in the matter of the vote. The heroines of these novels, such as Sybylla in Franklin's *My Brilliant Career* or Hervey in Jameson's *Mirror in Darkness*, emerge individually into equality with men, rather than developing with other women a collective opposition to the subjection of women by men.

Some of the novels by women in which the narrator concentrates on male politics, particularly the clash between left- and right-wing forces, are also centred on a heroine who seeks equality with men. An example of this kind of mixture of male and female politics occurs in Storm Jameson's trilogy, *Mirror in Darkness*. In this work, the narrator tries for a panoramic view of class politics in Britain after 1918, including the depiction of harrowing scenes such as the death of an undernourished small boy, Clive, in his cockroach-infested basement, and Frank Rigby's loss of employment as a bus-driver subsequent to the 1926 General Strike. This portrayal of class poverty and power politics is anodyne, however, in comparison with the characterisation of Hervey Russell, who engages in 'sexual politics', not as a feminist might, but as one of those exceptional women who make close friends only with men, competing with them on her own terms, even to the point of giving up the intimate mothering of her son.

Hervey, a journalist and novelist, exists on the fringe of a group of male socialists and other radicals who become involved in either fostering or negotiating an end to a fictionalised version of the actual 1926 General Strike. Apart from Hervey, most of the other women characters tend to fall in with the demands of their men and their children. Rachel, for example, wife of the socialist MP, Louis Earlham, criticises her husband's lukewarm socialism and, at the same time, cannot see how she retreats from politics into the nurture of her two young children. Frank Rigby's wife endures working-class poverty dutifully. But Hannah, Renn's lover, is an exception, like Hervey, among these domesticated women:

> 'I'm only twenty-one and all my life is to come. I must be free to take what comes. I don't want to marry and perhaps have children, yet. I want to see Vienna and Paris, I want all the things the world has to give, I want to swallow the whole of life in one long gulp. Even if it disappoints me I want to taste it.'[4]

But Hannah is not a putative feminist like Hervey who wants equal opportunities with men. Instead she wants to exploit and enjoy her sexual attraction towards and for men as fully as possible. The narrator, despite identifying possible ways to freedom for women, is blind to the anomaly of women taking little part in political or social action.

In Kylie Tennant's *Tiburon* (1935), some women take part in a 1930s strike in which the unemployed refuse to 'scab' on other unskilled labourers, and therefore do not take jobs offered at a lower rate of pay than that agreed by the majority of such labourers. But it is the men who strike, and the women who dole out soup to the unemployed who are refused relief, that is, unemployment benefit.

But in Katherine Susannah Prichard's goldfields' trilogy, *The Roaring Nineties* (1946), *Golden Miles* (1948), and *Winged Seeds* (1950), which is partly an historical reconstruction of events on the West Australian goldfields from 1892 onwards, central female characters such as Nadya Owen and Sally Gough are not only working wives and mothers, but also become political reformers who work with male radicals in order to bring about change.

Prichard's trilogy is exceptional in its portrayal of women who are active in trade union politics.

Jean Devanny's *Cindie* (1949), which is of that same period and is also set in a masculine working world – that of sugar plantation life in Queensland – is not so adventurous in its presentation of its eponymous heroine. Cindie is the equal of any male manager, but she is not shown actively engaging in politics. Nevertheless, the Australian Communist Party disliked the narrator's account of labour relations between Europeans and Kanakas (Melanesians) and their disapproval led to Devanny's resignation from that Party.

The hostility of the Party leadership was probably a reaction to comments by the narrator on, for example, the racialism of socialists: 'In respect of its White Australia policy based on racial discrimination, nothing separated the Australian Labour Movement from the most reactionary of the big moneyed men represented by the tories.'[5] The characterisation of the heroine, Cindie, might also have alienated these Party readers. Cindie is egalitarian in her attitude to other races, including aborigines. When asked by her friend, Jeff, how she managed to get the aborigines to fell trees for her when most of the other station-owners and managers could not get them to work consistently at any labouring job, she replied, 'I simply treat them exactly the same as I treat white men. The same as Mr. Biddows [the owner of the station which she managed] treats the Kanakas.'[6] Cindie competes successfully with men in sugar plantation management, which strikes a fictional blow against the sexism of macho outback men then and now.

The novels of Christina Stead span almost the entire century. Some of her fiction both early and late reflects as well as subverts changing reactions to women by men, and by women to each other. In her first novel, *Seven Poor Men of Sydney* (1934), for example, in which the narration is centred on male politics in the period from just prior to the First World War until the 1920s, one of the main characters, Baruch, makes a telling comment on the status of women:

'There are no women . . . There are only dependent and exploited classes, of which women make one. The peculiarities are imposed on them to keep them in order. They are told from the cradle to the grave, You are a female and not altogether there, socially and politically: your brain is good but not too good, none of your race was ever a star, except in the theatre. And they believe it. We all believe these great social dogmas.'[7]

Thus the narrator, through Baruch's simplistic exaggerations, is putting across one of the more neglected aspects of political feminism: how to make an analysis of women's subjection by men in relation to subjection according to class. Women, however, although under subjection, are not actually in a class of their own, but in an underrated grouping according to gender, which cuts across all classes.

Stead's narrator also demonstrates how, in the 1930s, both men and women found 'dogmas' such as the notion that women are in some ways inferior to men hard to give up, especially those who enjoyed the unpaid services of women. Milt Dean, for example, in response to Baruch's statement, defends what he believes is 'feminine':

> 'Where would be feminine charm? . . . I don't want to marry some big husky who shouts orders to wharfingers six hours a day. I want a woman who waits for me at home, who knows how to arrange knick-knacks, who gives me children and wants to bring them up for me, to teach them at her knees, to look after me in sickness, to close my eyes in death.'[8]

But a woman could just as easily utter such platitudes in reverse about her partner. In this novel, both sides to the question of women's rights and women's subjection are presented through various characters by the concealed narrator, and the reader can draw her own conclusions.

Although the narrator makes no direct statements about women's participation in this male political world, the lives of two ineffectual female revolutionaries, Catherine Baguenault and Marion Folliot, indirectly comment on the disproportionate lack of power exerted by women in the male political world. Catherine falls in and out of love with various radical men, as well as espousing good works, and Marion, the wife of one of the leading Communists, Fulke Folliott, flirts with all the radical males she meets. These women try to use men to meet their sexual needs, rather than to attempt to co-operate politically with them.

Cotters' England (1967), which brings us into the era of the beginning of 1960s feminist collectivism, or what might be called 'second wave feminism', takes an ironic view of post-1960 left-wing women who unite politically. Her anti-heroine, Nellie Cotter, is portrayed as developing a cynical, man-parodying lust for power over women which leads her to bring about a young woman's suicide. Nellie gives an all-women week-end party at her own home in her husband's absence:

> The guests began to come from their work. Some would not be free till the next day. They were all working women . . . Nellie's rough gang, women of forty or thereabouts, all hard workers, but too tough, even depraved and licentious, who lived like disorderly men . . . They talked about political chances, news of the day, Fleet Street secrets, journalists who had lost their jobs . . .[9]

The narrator indirectly criticises these characters for their lack of femininity, and in her comparison of them with 'disorderly men' she suggests that if women are allowed to become equal to men at work, then their behaviour will become as anti-life as that of men in similar work.

Nellie is the most depraved of all these women: she encourages Caroline, who lives with Nellie and her husband, to try to sleep during the party, on the pretext that sleeping during the party will help her with her persistent insomnia. Then Nellie terrorises her:

> She had a moment of excruciating fear. She saw in a moment that it was Nellie dressed in an airman's suit and that her open gash of a mouth was smiling and that her long hand had beckoned her. She had a thought that Nellie meant her some harm in the room, even to kill her. Nellie moved over and was standing stooping under the skylight, and nodded to her to come in: she smiled like a clown in the moonshade. Caroline went and stood on the box Nellie showed her and looked out from the skylight first at the late light of the sky and then down, down said the nod and the finger, into the back yard . . .
>
> A number of naked women were rounding, breaking, wrestling, weaving together in the back yard between the brick walls, the high fence and the tree. The moonlight showed that some were rosy in the daytime, others were the colors of night-lighted fish and they were like queer fish, a seahorse, an old man snapper, a gar, a toadfish, a puffball and one rather awkward and hesitant was as yet, only a woman: and what was more ludicrous, partly dressed.[10]

The narrator's transmogrification of the naked women – seen through Caroline's point of view – into various types of 'queer fish' hints at the seamier side of some lesbian behaviour; the female seahorse, for example, reverses sexual roles and implants the male with its young.

Caroline is afraid of Nellie's attempts to get her to join in the nude dancing and runs off. But she broods over Nellie's earlier insinuations about Caroline's destiny:

> 'The Bride-of-Death. That would be something glorious to experience, the last submission, the splendid last breath, the sacred swoon . . . It would be a great and glorious thing if one of us turned out to have a soul of that quality: I always thought it might be you, Caroline.'[11]

Caroline becomes convinced that suicide is her destiny and jumps to her death from a tall block to the ground below. Thus Nellie, who has been unable to acquire much power in journalism or politics, creates for herself a perverse hold over Caroline. Nellie, the liberated woman who has equality with men in both politics and work, misuses her power in a way that is similar to that of corrupt men. If Nellie prefigures the late twentieth-century feminist, then women and men are shown to have equal potential for perverse wielding of power.

Meridel Le Sueur's *The Girl* (1978) also spans the 1930s to the 1970s, in that this novel was first written as a series of sketches in 1939 and rewritten in this published version in 1977–8. This first-person narration by 'the girl', which is presented by a covert narrator, subverts patriarchal conventions about the importance of virility as an adjunct to the exercise of masculine power over both women and weaker men. Through 'the girl's' eyes, we see the social, economic, and personal corruption that is brought about by the assertion of macho power.

The Girl is set during the period of the 1930s depression in a mid-western American town. Butch and Bill want to work, and are willing to scab on fellow workers who are on strike at the local foundry. When they turn up for work there on 'Blue Monday', Bill is shot and killed. Butch then gets involved with Ganz, a big-time crook who organises a bank raid in which 'the girl' is the driver of the getaway car. She agrees to their plan because she is pregnant by Butch and wants the stolen money so that they can get married. The raid turns into a fiasco: Butch shoots the other two gang members because they are running off with the loot, and is then wounded himself. 'The girl' helps Butch escape, but she is too frightened to seek medical treatment for fear of capture, and her lover dies.

This narrative is a send-up of romances about knights fighting valiantly for their true loves, since Butch only achieves a bank raid which goes wrong. And even if he had stolen money from the bank, he finds that his plan to start up a service station is just a chimera:

> O sure, . . . [the service station 'owner'] said, that's a racket, they make you feel like you got your place, like you're going to be the boss, a big shot. They take all your dough and they got it fixed so you can't make good . . . And when you give up, when they've sucked you dry, they get another sucker.
>
> Holy mackerel! Butch said . . . Oh, the Goddamned dirty bastards. They got you coming and going. They got you.[12]

Butch discovers that the state exploits its labourers in a way that is comparable to his sexual exploitation of 'the girl', whose sexual services he hired out to Ganz in order to get in with him on the bank raid.

'The girl' makes a critique of the state and its inability to provide a living for its physically able members: 'It was awful to see the four of them [Butch, Ganz, Hoinck and Ack, the bank robbers] like drowning men from a rotting ship slanting out together, each one alone but in some terrible violence hanging together.'[13] The 'rotting ship' resembles the society which refuses them a livelihood, despite their attempts to prove themselves as courageous macho men. Butch, for example, wants to marry and to support his wife and child but society denies him the opportunity to work.

After the central male characters have killed each other in the abortive bank-raid, some of the women unite politically in the Workers Alliance – a women's collective which resembles the consciousness-raising groups of women in the 1960s and 1970s. When Clara dies of anaemia, the Alliance organises a mass demonstration:

> Amelia said – Yes a Memorial for Clara, a mass meeting, let our voice be heard in the whole city – a trial, a judgement against the city fathers, a trial, yes an accusation. We accuse. Yes, we point a finger. We hold them responsible . . . Clara is dead. Who killed Clara? Why didn't she have milk and iron pills? Who didn't care if she died? . . . *Who will kill us?*
>
> O it was something to hear and see this anger. And their power. Amelia looked like the mother of them all, nodding, smiling.[14]

In this litany of accusation, patriarchal 'get-rich-quick' crimes are indicted, crimes which are usually committed by men.

Some post-1960s fiction shows a marked change from what went before in both themes and characterisation. Barbara Wilson's *Ambitious Women* (1988) and Nicky Edwards's *Mud* (1986) are illustrative examples of this new kind of women's fiction which, like *The Girl*, gets to grips with problems of both class and sexual politics. Women who engaged with men in class politics in the 1960s are shown in *Ambitious Women* as having become disenamoured of male-oriented political demonstrations:

> 'Maybe I got tired of male politics after I realized that that's all they were – male politics. The Revolution could come and go, but I began to see that it wasn't in the plan for women to enjoy the fruits of equality and freedom from oppression.'[15]

Here Denver expresses one of the main disagreements between socialist and separatist Marxist feminists: some feminists co-operate with male socialists in order to bring about political change, and others assert that, because socialist men are as oppressive as any other men, they need to work towards political change for women separately.

The male characters in *Ambitious Women* – ex-husbands and friends of the three central female characters – are represented as egotistical and dominating. Allison's ex-husband, Tom, for example, had used various methods of getting his own way in their marriage:

> in her own marriage, middle-class to the core in spite of their student poverty, physical violence would have been unthinkable. Tom had other ways of keeping her compliant and they always ran to the underground, withholding technique. Silence, no sex, or quiet threats of separation. 'If you don't like the way I am, Alli,' he would say, 'there's no reason for us to stay together.' Putting the burden on her to decide to go her own way (with two children, of course), plumping the myth that they were rational, free adults, instead of a woman and a man bound together by numerous economic ties, including the maintenance of two small children. She never would have left him, so fearful was she, so needy of a husband, he had to leave her before she could realize (but had she ever really realized?) that she could make it on her own. No, he had never had to beat her to make her see things his way. Why, indeed, ever resort to physical violence, when, like Tom, you held someone's life in your hands like the puppet master holding a cross-stick and wire?[16]

Once Tom has left her, Allison is able to pressure him into arranging loans for her to start up a business of her own, but, as her business partner, Holly, observes, Allison is never able to kick the habit of playing the role of the somewhat 'stupid' woman whenever her ex-husband visits her.

Holly's husband, James, whom she left because he was addicted to drugs and attacked her physically, is a Vietnam war veteran. But the narrator has a blind spot to men's problems and thus does not show how James is also a victim of a patriarchal system that has propagated war in a foreign country for doubtful political motives. Paul, the semi-appendage of the third female lead character, Magda, who is portrayed as supportive of women to a limited extent. When Magda, who has published an interview with a member of the radical political group, the Cutting Edge, is summoned to appear before a grand jury investigation into the criminal activities of this group, Paul is sympathetic. Nevertheless, he tries to assert his superiority as a journalist, telling Magda that he could have written up this subversive interview with more political nous than she. Magda inwardly disagrees: '. . . why couldn't he keep his mouth shut? He had to keep asking her why she hadn't been harder on Deb in the interview . . . just where did he get off criticizing Magda's questions when he would never, never have the guts to do what she'd done?'[17] Thus Magda asserts, not her equality with her fellow male journalist and former lover, but her superiority to him.

Ambitious Women is concerned more with the politics of gender than with class, so that the possibility of a radical class upheaval, which is hinted at by the politics of the Cutting Edge, however reprehensible the violence of their methods, is scarcely adumbrated in the narration. Nicky Edwards's *Mud* might be read as a subversion of patriarchal beliefs in the efficacy of warfare to settle disputes, but such subversion is only partial: the narrator is blind to the distinction between the elder male who dominates and the younger male who is dominated, particularly in wartime.

Jo, the first-person narrator, is writing a play in which the politics of the First World War are challenged by those of contemporary feminists at Greenham Common. At the Imperial War Museum, Jo confronts a 'ghost' from the First World War, John, the dead husband of the old-age pensioner, Ada, who has agreed to give Jo a first-hand account of her experience of the First World War. Jo treats the 'ghost' dismissively, mainly because he is male:

'He's all right,' he reached for the diary I had been working from earlier. His hands were long and bloodless-looking. 'Bit pious, mind, but not bad.'

'Look, piss off, will you?' I turned around in my chair to give him the full benefit of my space-defending glare. He looked like an American, with his short hair parted in the middle and his little moustache, but sounded like a Londoner. Early twenties, I would have said, except for the lines of strain around his eyes. Not quite all there.

'I'm sorry,' he looked more puzzled than hurt. The permanent comprehension gap of the unwanted male.[18]

Whether readers find the 'ghost of the Great War past' convincing or not, the narrator's description of Jo's attitude to him exemplifies a lack of perception of the way in which militarism underlies all patriarchal systems of government and in time of war oppresses young men as much as if not more than young women.

The narrator portrays Jo reading the 'diary' of the long-dead John, but the knowledge she gains about the way in which John had been victimised by a military tribunal at which the lies of a superior officer were preferred to the truth told by John, a private, is not shown as bringing about a changed point of view in Jo. She still criticises him for subscribing to the patriarchal ideal of protecting his wife, Ada, from the truth about his court-martial for cowardice, without realising that John himself has been a victim of patriarchal incompetence, not only at the court-martial, but through his death in war.

When Jo encounters her 'ghost' of John (which seems to be a device used by the external narrator to convey Jo's anti-male fantasies) for the last time, she rejects his angry plea that she try to understand why he had never wanted his wife to know he had been court-martialled:

'You take yourself too seriously,' I said, brutally. And what an understatement.

'It's for her,' he sounded surprised, resentful. 'I want to protect her.'

'Bullshit.'

'You don't understand.' He was seething . . .

'Listen, mate,' I was getting angry myself now, 'you may have some trouble with this concept, but I'm a radical feminist and I'm not taking orders from any damn man. Living or otherwise. So you can take your doomy spectral utterances and stick them.'[19]

The 'ghost' has been constructed as a symbolic scapegoat into which

Jo can stick her anti-male pins, rather than as a technique for reconstructing the ideological milieu of the First World War.

In contrast, the contemporary women's political scene is well-dramatised in *Mud*: the dogmas of Greenham Common protesters are set against those of a group of way-out feminists who believe that the Greenham Common women are wasting energy that would be better spent on improving women's lot *vis-à-vis* men. Jo, who spent a year camping at Greenham, is shown arguing her case for Greenham against a group of anti-Greenham feminists:

> 'A real live peace woman,' Connie murmured. 'In probably the only right-on household in London that doesn't want to save the mother earth for generations of unborn little pink babies.'
> 'They come in other shades than pink, you know,' I snapped. There was a sense of gears changing, real disagreements about to come out. 'And why not save the world, anyway? You got a death wish?'
> 'Because it's full of shit. Here and now.' Jess was definitely not into keeping it civilized. 'It's a fucking awful world, full of women getting fucked over and you want to save it just as it is for men to carry on like they always have.'[20]

And so on. Women who protest against the danger to civilisation of nuclear power and nuclear bombs are starting their revolution to change male behaviour at one end of the scale of its mismanagement. Feminists who are antipathetic to the nuclear protesters want to change masculine misbehaviour wherever it occurs.

An earlier novel which was published during the last year of the First World War, Rebecca West's *The Return of the Soldier* (1918), carries a more subtle critique of patriarchal mismanagement during that war than does Nicky Edwards's *Mud*. Through the characterisation of the officer, Chris Baldry, who has returned so shocked by his experience that he suffers complete amnesia for the events of the past fifteen years, the narrator implies the horror of that war. The character who actually relates the tale as a participant observer, Jenny Baldry – the cousin of the main protagonist – shows a vivid awareness of the terrors of the front line at a time when such information was supposed to have been censored, both officially and unofficially. Here she relates her dreams:

> Of late I had had bad dreams about him. By night I saw Chris running across the brown rottenness of No Man's Land, starting back here

because he trod upon a hand, not even looking there because of the awfulness of an unburied head, and not till my dream was packed full of horror did I see him pitch forward on his knees as he reached safety – if it was that. For on the war-films I have seen men slip down as softly from the trench parapet, and none but the grimmer philosophers would say that they had reached safety by their fall . . .

Well, such are the dreams of Englishwomen to-day; I could not complain.[21]

In the final sentence, 'I could not complain', the first-person narrator demonstrates her ambivalence about the destructive war that she is living through vicariously. On the one hand, she portrays the 'horror' of No Man's Land with extreme disapproval as well as distaste, but, on the other hand, she accepts the then stereotyped view that she should not make any overt criticism of that war.

Yet, throughout this novel, the narrator covertly criticises the conduct of the war which leads to the physical and mental destruction of young men. Chris's total amnesia for the events of the past fifteen years is shown to have been an unconscious reaction to war as a way of escaping from that war:

They could not take him back to the Army as he was . . . he had raised an appalled face from the pages of a history of the war. 'Jenny, it can't be true – that they did *that* – to Belgium? Those funny, quiet, stingy people . . .' And his soldierly knowledge was as deeply buried as this memory of that awful August . . . they could not send him back into the hell of war.[22]

If war is hell, then why support it? In the characterisation of Jenny, the narrator does not broach this question. But, at the conclusion of the novel, again we have an implied criticism of those who help to return 'shell-shocked' soldiers to so-called normality; in other words, to a state of mind in which they are again willing to participate in the mechanism of war, and thus willing to fight and kill other men with the latest technological inventions.

Chris is cured of his amnesia by Margaret, the love of his youth, with whom he has got in touch as if the fifteen years since they parted during a lover's quarrel had never taken place. After he had broken off with Margaret, Chris had taken on his father's business and estate, married and had a child who had died at the age of two. In a discussion with Chris's psychiatrist. Margaret realises that emotional reminders of this boy will almost certainly nudge him from his emotional fixation at a point fifteen years earlier. She is loath to bring about this regaining of memory, however, since she knows that his romantic attachment to her will then be replaced by his legal and affectional ties with his wife, Kitty. Nevertheless, she takes to him items of the dead boy's clothing, because 'The truth's the truth . . . and he must know it'.[23] As predicted, Chris is jolted into a state of full recall:

> Chris walked across the lawn. He was looking up under his brows at the overarching house as though it were a hated place to which, against all his hopes, business had forced him to return . . . He wore a dreadful decent smile; I knew how his voice would resolutely lift in greeting us. He walked not loose limbed like a boy, as he had done that very afternoon, but with the soldier's hard tread upon the heel. It recalled to me that, bad as we were, we were not yet the worst circumstance of his return. When we had lifted the yoke of our embraces from his shoulders he would go back to that flooded trench in Flanders under that sky more full of flying death than clouds, to that No Man's Land where bullets fall like rain on the rotting faces of the dead . . .[24]

Thus the title of the novel refers primarily, not to the actual return of 'the soldier' from the front, but to Chris's return from the complete oblivion of amnesia to a world of reality that includes 'the yoke' of his womenfolk as well as that of the Army.

The first-person narrator's phrase, 'the yoke of our embraces', reveals another curious dichotomy in her mind: she sees cultivated attractive women like herself and Chris's wife, Kitty, as simultaneously necessary to yet parasitical on patriarchal society. Here Kitty is about to meet the psychiatrist who indirectly brings about her husband's cure:

> . . . for this moment she was glowing. I knew it was because she was going to meet a new man and anticipated the kindling of admiration in his eyes . . . Beautiful women of her type lose, in this matter of admiration alone, their otherwise tremendous sense of class distinction; they are obscurely aware that it is their civilizing mission to flash the jewel of their beauty before all men, so that they shall desire it and work to get the wealth to buy it, and thus be seduced by a present appetite to a tilling of the earth that serves the future. There is, you know, really room for all of us; we each have our peculiar use.[25]

This last sentence might seem an attempt at irony, since to stimulate men's sexual longings merely to frustrate them is a useless procedure. But in the context of the remainder of the novel, the narrator is here presenting Jenny's view that her sister-in-law, as well as she herself, are of some use to society even though they contribute nothing to the economy but are instead a burden on the man who keeps them. Elsewhere the narrator, through her straight presentation of Jenny's views, of which she shows no disapproval, reveals a denigration of working-class and working women which is occasionally tinged with an attempt to discover their common humanity.

The attitude to the working classes that dominates this novel is that they can never rise from the unlovely and impoverished position in which their class membership places them. Nevertheless this attitude is occasionally ameliorated by moments of insight, as when, for example, Kitty is shown to be a vain and self-indulgent creature in contrast with Margaret and her compassionate behaviour:

> She [Margaret] was repulsively furred with neglect and poverty, as even a good glove that has dropped down behind a bed in a hotel and has lain undisturbed for a day or two is repulsive when the chambermaid retrieves it from the dust and fluff . . . Yet there was something about the physical quality of the woman, unlovely though she was, which preserved the occasion from utter baseness . . . It was, strangely enough, only when I looked at Kitty and marked how her brightly coloured prettiness arched over this plain criminal, as though she were a splendid bird of prey and this her sluggish insect food, that I felt the moment degrading.[26]

The first-person narrator oscillates between implying that the incomparably beautiful Kitty is mean spirited and presenting her as the epitome of ideal womanhood. By the conclusion of the novel, working-class Margaret is shown to be capable of disinterested self-sacrifice, in contrast with upper-class Kitty, 'who was in tune with every kind of falsity'.[27] These conflicting world-views in the novel reflect the shake-up in women's conception of themselves which occurred at the close of the First World War. The first-person narrator, Jenny Baldry, questions both Kitty's and her own economic position in society, suggesting that, as 'kept women', they are a burden to the man who supports them.

The history of women's conflicting attitudes to feminism during the twentieth century can be traced more or less through fiction written by women. On the one hand, this century abounds in politically conservative novels by women, from *Mrs Dalloway* to *Hotel du Lac*, in which the narrator seeks to preserve the *status quo* of men on the whole taking on the major part of the prestigious roles in society and women servicing men in these roles. And, on the other hand, we can discover throughout this century a small number, from *My Brilliant Career* to *Mud*, of women's radical novels.

Fiction by women in the last two decades, however, has begun to broach openly the political problems of living in a society which has been called by some a 'post-feminist world'. Whether we accept this description of the effects of 'second wave feminism' or not, women novelists have recently been trying to give women readers a chance to read about contemporary society from the point of view of women who seek to bring about change in both the metaphorical and legal status of women.

7

Beyond racial stereotypes

The representation by male authors of relations between European women and black men in fiction is often stereotypically favourable to the imaginative interests of men. V. S. Naipaul's *The Mimic Men* (1967), for example, epitomises a masculine conception of a mixed-race marriage in which the female European partner, Sandra, is portrayed as the cynical and knowing vamp, who entraps sexually the naive and misguided Indian student narrator:

> She had failed a qualifying examination for the second time. That was the end of her government grant, the end of the School. No degree for her now; no escape by that route . . . What awaited her? The secretarial course, the librarian's course, the common employer. She went on, railing at her society, bitter at her lack of protection and patrons within it. A job in the bank; the typing pool; the Woolworth's counter. She was working herself up to a pitch of hysteria. Tears of anger came to her eyes. Then suddenly, fixing those moist eyes on me, she said, almost ordered, with a look of total hatred: 'Why don't you propose, you *fool*?' . . . for the first time since our talk had begun, I thought of her painted breasts.[1]

The first-person narrator initially presents himself as exploited by Sandra, who wants a position and financial security in life. But when he returns to the fictional island of Isabella in the West Indies with his English bride, he recounts what might be considered a stock melodrama of the gradual dissolution of a marriage that has been based, from the narrator's point of view, on concupiscence. Sandra, who has affairs in the same way as her husband, is portrayed as pitiable, whereas the narrator generally sees himself as on top – metaphorically if not always literally – of the West Indian and European women with whom he engages sexually.

On the other hand, Ruth Prawer Jhabvala in *Three Continents* (1987), invents a young first-person narrator, Harriet, an American of European descent, who becomes drugged, as it were, by her experience of sexuality with an Indian conman, Crishi. Harriet is willing to submit to any kind of neglect in order that she might again experience sexual orgasm with her lover and subsequent husband:

> He had aroused me so completely that the sex he gave me – rationed out to me – was absolutely essential to me. Deprived of it, I was as if without breath and air. Really sometimes I lay there in such an agony of unfulfilled longing, I was fighting for breath. I was hardly a person anymore but just this fearful *need*. It is shaming to write this – to have allowed myself to be so overcome. I was furious with him when he didn't turn up, but when he did I flung myself on him in a fury of desire. I tore at him, I literally did. I was a starved animal and he laughed and liked it. I had no defenses at all – against him, against myself, against this sex.[2]

Even when other characters, such as the Bari Rani, enlighten her about the criminal nature of Crishi's involvement with the supposedly radical semi-religious movement, 'Transcendental Internationalism', Harriet's sexual drive and desire for its fulfilment make her suppress any knowledge of how she is being exploited financially and emotionally. Harriet, throughout this novel, is the willing victim of corrupting Crishi, and her naïveté in the face of knowledge about his present and past crimes is not entirely convincing, despite the detailed descriptions of the lust which she claims overpowers her. At the conclusion, she even connives with Crishi over concealing the murder of her twin brother, Michael, in order that Crishi might be given, not only Harriet's wealth, but also her brother's.

This theme of the European woman who, primarily because she does not want to lose her feeling of being sexually fulfilled, cannot disengage herself from an unsuitable Indian partner, is also central to Jhabvala's earlier *Heat and Dust* (1975). The first-person narrators in *Heat and Dust* and *Three Continents* imply for the European reader that the myth that Indian men are more skilled than Europeans at pleasing women sexually – or at least arousing them – has some basis in fact. But both these narrators are unreliable in that their addiction to sexual coition blinds them to other aspects of 'reality'. Since these narrators do not represent Jhabvala's own world-view, she could be said to be exposing this sexual stereotype for our consideration. In other fiction, she presents a variety of different viewpoints.

In some of her stories in her collection, *How I Became a Holy Mother* (1976), Jhabvala concentrates for example, on both sexual and asexual relationships between Indian women and men. Pritam, the main character of 'In the Mountains', represents the Indian woman who is sated with modern open sexuality, and seeks isolation and celibacy at a mountain retreat. But her state of meditative solitude becomes enhanced by a platonic friendship with an eccentric man. Pritam's conventional mother longs for her daughter to engage in 'a proper life like everybody else', which in contemporary India means concupiscent sexuality. Pritam's mother, however, is shown eventually coming round to acceptance of her daughter's celibacy: 'She could not deny that Pritam was different . . . People admired her and thought it a fine thing that a girl could be so emancipated in India and lead a free life, just as in other places.'[3] What is implied here is that conventional Indians like Pritam's mother think that a woman living 'a free life, just as in other places' is somewhat absurd if such women deny their sexuality. Yet if supposedly more emancipated societies allow women to choose celibacy, these Indian women will go along with what to them is an odd choice for a woman.

In another story, 'Desecration', the theme of women who become addicted to debased sexual practices is again taken up, but, unlike both *Heat and Dust* and *Three Continents*, here the main character is a young Indian woman in relationships with men from her own race. Sofia, a conventional young married woman, is so stifled that, like Flaubert's Madame Bovary, she resorts to immorality and sexual self-abasement in order to relieve her boredom. She is married to Raja Sahib who is thirty years older than she is. Unlike Pritam, she cannot convert her sexual dissatisfaction into meditative philosophy, but engages sexually with a roué, the local Superintendent of Police, Bakhtawar Singh, who gradually debases her:

> Sofia was his first girl of good family. Her refinement intrigued him . . . As their intimacy progressed, he also made her perform acts that he had learned from prostitutes. It seemed that he could not reach far enough into her, physically and in every other way.[4]

When finally Singh begins to tire of her, she longs to confess her pain to her husband, but she is afraid that he will reject her:

There had never been anyone in the world who looked into her eyes the way he did, with such love but at the same time with a tender respect that would not reach farther into her than was permissible between two human beings. And it was because she was afraid of changing that look that she did not speak. What if he should turn aside from her, the way he had when she had asked forgiveness for the drunken servant?[5]

Sofia's suicide in the hotel room in which she used to meet her debaucher – a suicide which the narrator has announced in the first paragraph – is thus explained. But, through this juxtaposition of Sofia's desire for love with her acquiescence in lust, the narrator indirectly comments on the position of women who have no outlet in their shut-in homes for their emotional self-expression.

Many of the problems for women, whether they come from European or other cultures, are inherent in their sexuality and the possibility that society allows for its expression. Padma Perera, like Jhabvala, also explores in fiction the two alternatives for Indian women: marriage or celibacy. In 'Pilgrimage' (1978), one of the stories that make up Perera's collection, *Birthday Deathday* (1985), Eknath makes a pass at his young stepmother who rejects it. When his father dies, Eknath tells her, 'You are nearer my age than his. It was not right, it was not proper.' His stepmother explains her social position:

'You live in your world of ideas, what can you know of hunger and poverty and the pain of being a woman? My father was ill. There was no money for either medicine or food.'
'You mean my father bought you?'
In the silence he heard her catch her breath. 'Don't you see,' she said. 'Better your father than some evil old landlord or moneylender.'[6]

Eknath's stepmother, now she is widowed, takes refuge in an *ashram*, which in India is a form of traditional retirement for widows. Eknath, however, is no better off. After his second rejection by his stepmother, he relinquishes his promising career as a newspaper cartoonist, and spends his life travelling from one place to another. In this story, men are shown as entrapped in false social roles as are women.

Another theme which is common to fiction about the mixing of ethnic backgrounds and cultures is that of the immigrant from the East who tries to live in the Western world. In Perera's 'Weather Report',[7] an Indian woman tells her own story about her incarceration in and eventual escape from an arranged marriage. Her difficulties are compounded because she and her possessive husband have emigrated to America. But she learns Spanish at evening classes, adopts the name of Conchita Perez, leaves her husband, and takes a bus to New Mexico, where she intends to disappear. Perhaps this escape is the only possible one in *ashram*-less America which expects a man-less woman to fend for herself.

In the work of Jean Rhys, who was of Welsh descent but born and brought up in the West Indies, we find a partial exploration of the problems of West Indian women who emigrate to London. In her short story, 'Let Them Call it Jazz' (1962), she attempts to fabricate a West Indian dialect for the first-person narrator, unemployed Selina Davis, who inadvertently ends up in Holloway women's prison. This narration is sustained in a speech pattern that echoes West Indian forms without mimicking them. In the following episode, for example, Selina is retrieved from hopelessness by the 'Holloway song':

> It's a smoky kind of voice, and a bit rough sometimes, as if those old dark walls theyselves are complaining, because they are too much misery – too much. But it don't fall down and die in the courtyard; seems to me it could jump the gates of the jail easy and travel far, and nobody could stop it. I don't hear the words – only the music . . .
> When I'm back in my cell I can't just wait for bed. I walk up and down and I think. 'One day I hear that song on trumpets and these walls will fall and rest.' I want to get out so bad I could hammer on the door, for I know now anything can happen, and I don't want to stay lock up here and miss it.[8]

Selina finds her voice and explains to the prison medical officer how she had been provoked into throwing a stone through a window. He facilitates her release. Holloway gaol has hardened her relations with society: she lies her way into employment, and when a man steals her 'Holloway song' music, she rapidly recovers:

> I get a letter from him telling me he has sold the song and as I was quite a help he encloses five pounds with thanks.
> I read the letter and I could cry. For after all, that song was all I had . . .
> Now I've let them play it wrong . . .
> But then I tell myself all this is foolishness. Even if they played it on trumpets, even if they played it just right . . . no walls would fall so soon

. . . let them play it wrong. That won't make no difference to the song I heard.[9]

Selina's dialect is a successful modification of West Indian speech patterns, and Selina's cynicism about the fact that 'no walls would fall so soon' suggests the effect that prison might have on a naive newcomer to London.

In Maureen Duffy's *Wounds* (1969), the narrator fabricates the dialect of a West Indian woman in London, mother of two boys and deserted by her husband. In this passage, she meditates on the reasons for her British student lover's rejection of her:

> Why hadn't he come again? These people all the same, lead you on till you think you there and then and then. But he wasn't like that or at least she couldn't believe it though she told him again and again, 'It's always the same. You think people here are being kind and they are only being polite,' hating herself for saying it, for pushing out the plea toward him, the demand that he would have to answer, meaning, 'You, you. What went wrong? What happened?' Nothing had happened. That was the whole point. When it should have broken into multicoloured flares on the dark, the moment had fizzled damply and gone out and he wouldn't come again.[10]

This internal monologue from a West Indian woman who feels cut off from the dominant culture is convincing, although a patois is suggested, rather than its being modelled on an actual West Indian form of speech. The metaphor, 'multicoloured flares on the dark', is given in the third person voice of the narrator, and thus implies the imagery of the West Indian character's thought-processes.

Any technique for creating a character's voice depends, not on resurrecting material which stems from the author's own life, but on imagining a fictional human being who is believable. The knack of convincing the reader that the fictional voice is 'true' depends on the storyteller's ability to fabricate another person's voice and 'character', whatever the supposed race, class or gender of that 'character', or of the author. A particular author, in order to be convincing, does not need to belong to the race of the character that she is representing, as Jean Rhys's 'Let Them Call It Jazz', and her later historical novel, *Wide Sargasso Sea* (1976), illustrate. Moreover, a male author might construct a female character successfully, just as a female author might construct male characters who are convincing.

Joan Riley's *Waiting in the Twilight* (1987) gives the reader convincing males in the representation of the West Indian, Stanton, Adella's husband, and of the European estate agent:

> 'Why we caan see one a de other houses?'. . . [Adella] persisted.
> The . . . [estate agent] laughed uneasily, loosening his tie, as though it was suddenly too tight. 'Look, Mrs Johnson, most of those houses, well . . . they sell so fast. Many of them are gone before they even reach the papers.'
> Adella knew he was lying, even without the evidence of shifting eyes and increased perspiration . . .
> 'What about de one dem don't sell?' she insisted . . .
> The man moved uneasily, the ready smile fading from the red face, replaced by embarrassment. 'I am afraid some people are funny about just who they sell their houses to,' he muttered apologetically.
> She felt her mouth tighten at the evasive answer. Knew what he was really trying to say and she wanted to force him to admit that it was because she was black.[11]

The narrator without comment describes Adella's acceptance of the estate agent's clients' implicit rejection of blackness.

Nor does the narrator expose Stanton's masochistic toleration of the notion that any house will do for him because he is black. Stanton intervenes in the negotiations with the agent, even though it is Adella who has the money to buy a house:

> 'Can I take it you are interested?' the agent asked.
> Adella clutched her bag tightly, conscious of Stanton staring at her with bitter aggression, daring her to say no, after all he had been through. 'A interested, but a haffe tink about it,' she said, knowing that he sensed acceptance, yet needing to save her pride.
> 'When can you let us know?' the man pressed on. 'If I knew you were definitely interested, I could put a hold on it. Take it off the list, you know.'
> Who he trying to fool? she thought resentfully, nobody was going to line up to buy this thing. She was not going to let him push her . . . she felt a surge of irritation, when Stanton came back up the stairs.
> 'We'll tek it,' he said, looking apologetically at the man, before glaring at her.
> Adella flashed him a cold look. 'Is me money and a tink we should consider tings a bit before we sey anyting. We will get in touch like ihm say,' she finished, turning to the man; catching the hope fading from the light eyes.[12]

Here Adella is shown as up against the difficulties of being female as well as being black. Both her lack of clout as a woman and her acceptance of being discriminated against because of her race force her into buying the decaying house.

The narrator, however, represents Adella as a confirmed romantic, without exposing how such living in dreams is a flaw which will end in her self-defeat. Stanton beats her and the children regularly, and then deserts her for another woman, but Adella perpetually anticipates his return. On her death-bed she experiences a mystical vision of him:

> There was Stanton looking at her, wearing the same suit as in the picture. He had not aged at all, he was still the same and he was smiling the same smile she had always loved.
>
> 'A did sey yu would come back,' she said triumphantly. 'A did sey you wasn't goodfanuting'
>
> He stayed there, smiling, just smiling, and her mouth moved in a painful smile. It was hard to focus, but that was okay. Stanton was here now and nothing mattered . . .
>
> She heard him call her name again. Softly, in the secret way that was just between the two of them . . . Stanton had come back, just like she knew he would. He had come back and she had kept faith; and now he knew she had waited. The images flickered, faded slowly as her eyes dimmed.[13]

Adella can only face death by pretending that Stanton loved her despite his desertion of her. Since this novel is narrated from Adella's point of view, and since the third-person narrator tells her story without ironic comment, the truth of Adella's position is not exposed: that she has been dominated and ill-used by patriarchal West Indian and European men. This representation of her peaceful death is at odds with the sub-text which constructs an Adella who, because of her deprived background and lack of education, has lived miserably.

Joan Riley's first novel, *The Unbelonging* (1985), however, is uncompromisingly anti-romantic: when this novel opens, eleven-year-old Hyacinth is shown avoiding her father's attempts to molest her. Finally, when he tries to rape her, she runs away. But she finds she 'belongs' nowhere in Britain. The reception centre, the children's home, school, college, and even her university leave her restless and feeling out of place. She continually romanticises her hometown, Kingston, in Jamaica, and her aunt there. Yet, at the end of the novel, she finds that her fantasied 'happy' childhood in

Kingston had not been a continuous idyll, since she recalls how one of her friends had been burned to death by her 'mad' father in a household fire.[14] Hyacinth's fear of male sexuality becomes a focus of this novel in a way that is convincing. In both *Waiting in the Twilight* and in *The Unbelonging*, Riley's narrators are uncompromising about West Indian men's failings as husbands and fathers.

Alice Walker's fiction also portrays the disillusion of black women with their girlhood dreams, especially those about a male partner in life. Such disillusion occurs in her historical novel, *The Third Life of Grange Copeland*, which is set in the Deep South during the nineteenth century. At its opening, Margaret Copeland is beaten down by poverty as the wife of an indentured sharecropper, Grange. She takes to promiscuous sex as a form of escape. She is watched by her son, Brownfield, who finds her behaviour disturbing:

> Brownfield blamed his father for his mother's change. For it was Grange she followed at first . . . On some Saturday nights Grange and Margaret left home excitedly together, looking for Brownfield knew not what, except that it must be something strong and powerful and something they had thought lost . . . And even when Margaret found relief from her cares in the arms of her fellow bait-pullers and church members, or with the man who drove the truck and turned her husband to stone [the white farmer who treated them as slaves], there was a deference in her eyes that spoke of her love for Grange. On weekdays when, sober and wifely, she struggled to make food out of plants that grew wild and game caught solely in traps, she was submissive still. It was on weekends only that she became a huntress of soft touches, gentle voices and sex without the arguments over the constant and compelling pressures of everyday life.[15]

But Grange deserts her for the North, where he will at least escape serfdom if not poverty. Margaret kills herself because she cannot bear his loss: ' "Well. He's gone," his mother said without anger at the end of the third week. But the following week she and her poisoned baby [Brownfield's half-brother] went out into the dark of the clearing and in the morning Brownfield found them there.'[16] In this first generation – the 'first life' of Grange Copeland as husband and father – Margaret is the more or less passive dependant of Grange. In the next generation, Brownfield refuses the poverty his father has endured, only to become sexually enslaved to mother and daughter, Josie and Lorene, at the same time as he courts Mem, Josie's niece:

> . . . he stood it around the house as long as he could, screwing Josie and Lorene like the animal he felt himself to be, especially when he stood next day in the same room with Mem, whose heart, pained, was becoming readable in her eyes. There was no longer any joy in his conquest of these two women, for he had long since realized that *he* wasn't using them, *they* were using him . . .
>
> For a while it was grand being prize pawn; for both women, fast breaking from the strain of liquor, whoredom, money-making and battle, thought they truly loved him – but as a clean young animal they had not finished soiling. Their lives infinitely lacked freshness. They were as stale as the two-dollar rooms upstairs. Innocence continued to exist in him for them, since they were not able to see anything wrong in what they did with him. He enjoyed it and after all he was nobody's husband.[17]

Although this plot is far-fetched – Grange has also been Josie's lover even before his marriage to Margaret – the narrator makes the tragic outcome of Brownfield's upbringing psychologically convincing.

Brownfield marries Mem, a trained schoolteacher, but nevertheless his degradation progresses:

> Over the years they reached, what they would have called when they were married, an impossible, and *unbelievable* decline. Brownfield beat his once lovely wife now, regularly, because it made him feel, briefly, good. Every Saturday night he beat her, trying to pin the blame for his failure on her by imprinting it on her face; and she, inevitably, repaid him by becoming a haggard, automatous witch . . .
>
> For a woman like Mem, who had so barely escaped the 'culture of poverty', a slip back into that culture was the easiest thing in the world. First to please her husband, and then because she honestly could not recall her nouns and verbs, her plurals and singulars, Mem began speaking once more in her old dialect. The starch of her speech simply went out of her and what came out of her mouth sagged. . .[18]

What the narrator exposes here, is, in sociological terms, the 'double oppression' of women: Mem is an impoverished black sharecropper for a white farmer as well as being treated worse than a servant by her black husband. Brownfield's succumbing to depression about his life as a sharecropper is offered by the narrator as a psychological explanation of his crimes against Mem: 'in his depression he saw in his submissive, accepting wife a snare and a pitfall.'[19] This historical account of the lives of badly-done-by sharecroppers might be thought to have little to do with the way things are now, but the narrator of *The Third Life of Grange Copeland*, although drawing on the past for material, documents conditions which are parallel in some ways to our own: sex and money in our patriarchal society mean power for some and a kind of enslavement for others. Julia Kristeva suggests that 'what is repressed in discourse, in reproductive and productive relationships' can be called 'woman' or the 'oppressed social class' – 'it's the same struggle, and you never have one without the other'.[20]

In Walker's second novel, *Meridian* (1976), the recent Civil Rights movement in 1960s America is fictionalised in a way which links class and race struggles with the rise of 'second wave' feminism. This representation of recent history is achieved through the constructing of a black feminist, Meridian, who develops through this period a kind of mystical leadership, as shown in the following episode, in which she confronts small-town patriarchs:

> Standing with the children, directly opposite both the circus wagon and the tank, was Meridian, dressed in dungarees and wearing a light-colored, visored cap, of the sort worn by motormen on trains . . . With alarm, Truman [Meridian's friend] glanced at the tank in the center of the square. At that moment, two men were crawling into it, and a phalanx of police, their rifles pointing upward, rushed to defend the circus wagon . . .
> . . . when . . . [Meridian] reached the tank she stepped lightly, deliberately, right in front of it, rapped smartly on its carapace – as if knocking on a door – then raised her arm again. The children pressed onward, through the ranks of the arrayed riflemen and up to the circus car door. The silence, as Meridian kicked open the door, exploded in a mass exhalation of breaths, and the men who were in the tank crawled sheepishly out again to stare.[21]

Meridian thus asserts the rights of the town's black children to visit the circus wagon on *any* day, and not on a specific day reserved for blacks. But the narrator also suggests, by demonstrating the force of Meridian's moral power over the men in the tank, that if women stand up to men – whether they are metaphorical 'Hitlers' in public life or in the home – and defy their authority, men might become afraid to assert their superior physical power. Simone de Beauvoir, to quote a non-fictional parallel, has reported that women who assert power at work by striking are less submissive in the home.[22]

The narrator in this novel also deconstructs mid-twentieth-century black bourgeois marriage in which women are stifled. Ironically, for example, Meridian's mother is shown as having been destroyed by her marriage:

> [Meridian's mother] understood a look she saw in the other women's eyes. The mysterious inner life that she had imagined gave them [other mothers] a secret joy was simply a full knowledge of the fact that they were dead, living just enough for their children.[23]

When Meridian herself marries, the narrator reveals the low expectations black women hold for their husbands. Because Meridian believes 'old wives' tales' that forbid intercourse until three months after delivery of a baby, her husband turns to 'a woman who loved sex', so that he is able 'to get as much of it as he wanted every night'. Such behaviour is classified in the black women's community as 'good':

> He did not 'cheat' and 'beat' her both, which meant he was 'good' to her, according to her mother, his mother, the other women in the neighborhood and in fact just about everyone she knew, who seemed always to expect the two occurrences together, like the twin faces of a single plague.[24]

Meridian's husband leaves her, and Meridian joins the emerging Civil Rights movement of 1960.

In this novel, the narrator skilfully contrasts the historical past of slavery with the supposedly more liberal late twentieth century. Meridian's giving away of her small boy, for example, so that she can undertake a degree course at Saxon College is shown up by her ancestors' determination to keep their children and prevent them from being sold into slavery. And Meridian's act cannot be achieved without guilt:

> But she had not anticipated the nightmares that began to trouble her sleep. Nightmares of the child, Rundi, calling to her, crying, suffering unbearable deprivations because she was not there, yet she knew it was just the opposite: because she was not there he needn't worry, ever, about being deprived. Of his life, for instance. She felt deeply that what she'd done was the only thing, and was right, but that did not seem to matter. On some deeper level than she had anticipated or had even been aware of, she felt condemned, consigned to penitence, for life . . .

Meridian knew that enslaved women had been made miserable by the sale of their children, that they had laid down their lives, gladly, for their children, that the daughters of these enslaved women had thought their greatest blessing from 'Freedom' was that it meant they could keep their own children. And what had Meridian Hill done with *her* precious child? She had given him away. She thought of her mother as being worthy of this maternal history, and of herself as belonging to an unworthy minority, for which there was no precedent and of which she was, as far as she knew, the only member.[25]

The desire of mothers to keep their children has been socially constructed as almost universal, and the giving away of a child for adoption because the natural mother cannot bring her up herself is often fraught with guilt for the mother. Although here the narrator explicitly links Meridian's suffering with her knowledge of the history of her race, any female reader is likely to engage with Meridian's spiritual pilgrimage.

But the conclusion to *Meridian* is extraordinary in its presentation of her friend, Truman Held, taking over the spiritual mantle of leadership of the blacks from Meridian. After Meridian has been purged of the 'sin' of abandoning her child, Truman takes on her role of penitent:

[Meridian] was strong enough to go and owned nothing to pack. She had discarded her cap, and the soft wool of her newly grown hair framed her thin resolute face . . . Meridian would return to the world cleansed of sickness. That was what he knew . . .

It was his house now, after all, his cell. Tomorrow the people would come and bring him food. Someone would come and milk his cow. They would wait patiently for him to perform, to take them along the next guideless step. Perhaps he would . . .

Truman felt the room begin to turn and fell to the floor. A moment later he climbed shakily into Meridian's sleeping bag . . . and wondered if Meridian knew that the sentence of bearing the conflict in her own soul which she had imposed on herself – and lived through – must now be borne in terror by all the rest of them.[26]

The narrator implies that responsibility for what happens in any society must be borne by each of its members, and that individual 'sins' against others must be expiated before we can live peacefully with ourselves. These moral responsibilities apply equally to everyone, regardless of gender, race or class. Thus recent political history – the uniting of young men and women in the 1960s and

1970s in fighting for civil rights for black Americans and for the right to reject aggressive imperialism – is linked by the narrator with the belief that it is universally necessary for each person to make reparation for his or her own wrongdoing.

Walker's novels, such as *Meridian*, thus reflect universals by means of a recreation of a black person's experience of a dominantly European culture. The fiction by the white South African, Nadine Gordimer, however, although being concerned with conflict between Africans and Europeans, marginalises the issue of gender. In *Burger's Daughter* (1979), for example, the heroine, Rosa Burger, obtains an exit visa to visit France, and 'falls in love' with Bernard Chabalier, who is married with two children:

> I have asked him outright: you will have to make love to her [his wife] when you go home. We knew I meant . . . when I am living 'near by' the lycée and he has been with me. He never lies; and mine was a question only a foreign woman would ask, surely. I realize that. I feel no jealousy . . .[27]

Since this passage is narrated from Rosa's point of view, the reader must presume that she accepts the French ordering of social relations in which a 'mistress' is basically for male pleasure, but secondary to his wife who has official and legal status in the eyes of patriarchal law. The narrator offers no critique of this unjust arrangement for women.

But, since Rosa's 'love' for Chabalier is overthrown by her decision to return to South Africa and work with and for her black friends, it could be shown that the plot itself is imbued with the subversion of male authority. Thus, although the narrator accepts the ideal of 'romantic love', especially that between Rosa and Chabalier, such love is not sufficient for moral happiness: through Rosa, who ends up in prison for supposed political subversion of the State, women are shown as having a moral obligation to face truths about themselves and the culture in which they live, and to act accordingly.

In general, the European women characters who declaim in *Burger's Daughter* are not conscious of being oppressed by men. Flora Donaldson, for example, a political activist, sees only the oppression of black women, 'primarily by race and only secondarily by sex discrimination'.[28] Yet comments in this novel about the status of blacks could also be applied humorously to women, whether white or black; for example, when the African radical, Dhladhle says, 'All collaboration with whites has always ended in exploitation of blacks',[29] 'whites' could be replaced by 'men' and 'blacks' by 'women'. In another instance, when Rosa embraces her African friend, Marisa, false consciousness about race is compared with male tendencies to categorise women by their beauty or their lack of it:

> To touch in women's token embrace against the live, night cheek of Marisa, seeing huge for a second the lake-flash of her eye, the lilac-pink of her inner lip against translucent-edged teeth, to enter for a moment the invisible magnetic field of the body of a beautiful creature and receive on oneself its imprint – breath misting and quickly fading on a glass pane – this was to immerse in another mode of perception. As near as a woman can get to the transformation of the world a man seeks in the beauty of a woman.[30]

But for a man to seek 'beauty' in what is 'other' to himself is not commented upon by the narrator.

Olive Schreiner's *From Man to Man* (1926), which is less well-known than her *Story of an African Farm* (1883), is also set in South Africa. In this novel, condemnation of race and gender inequalities are treated as inseparable. Rebekah, for example, gradually develops an insight into and an ability to stand up to her philandering husband, Frank, an ability which goes hand in hand with her stance on the question of race. When she discovers that Frank is having sexual intercourse with their servant girl, she announces her wish to be free of him:

> for a moment he thought of bursting into a fit of rage such as had always silenced her . . .
> He was going to speak; he looked into her face, and a sense of something that seemed almost preternatural and inverted came over him. It was as if a man called to his own dog, who had followed him for years, and it walked by with its head down, no quiver even in its tail, and turned a dead eye on him.[31]

Rebekah then takes the child of her husband's liaison, Sartje, into her home, and encourages her children to treat her as their equal, even when she is called 'nigger' by their friends. When her sons refuse to walk openly with Sartje, she tells them:

'the day will come when you will regret utterly every slighting, every unkind word or act, that you have ever given place to towards Sartje, and when you will be deeply grateful for every kind or generous thing you have done towards her. Sartje is not a black child any more than she is pure white. It is not her fault that she is not white, any more than it is your virtue that you are not hálf black. Sartje is alone in the world. Her mother does not want her; her father does not know that he has even such a daughter in the world. She has no one but us to take care of her. I shall not ever ask one of you to walk with her again. She shall walk with me.'[32]

Yet political ideologies about gender and race which are implied in this novel here fall short in relation to the education of young boys about the nature of the sexual maltreatment of black servants. Rebekah does not tell her sons that Sartje is their half-sister, nor that their father has sexually misused his own black servant.

Ama Ata Aidoo in *Our Sister Killjoy* (1977) satirises various follies of men or women, including misconceptions and prejudices about race, class and gender. In the following passage, she mocks both 'moderate niggers' as well as pseudo-intellectuals:

What is frustrating, though, in arguing with a nigger who is a 'moderate' is that since the interests he is so busy defending are not even his own, he can regurgitate only what he has learnt from his bosses for you . . . The academic-pseudo-intellectual version is even more dangerous, who in the face of reality that is more tangible than the massive walls of the slave forts standing along our beaches, still talks of universal truth, universal art, universal literature and the Gross National Product.

Finally, when he has emptied his head of everything, he informs you solemnly that your problem is that you are too young. You must grow up.

Without doubt, the experience is like what a lover of chess or any mind-absorbing sport must feel who goes to a partner's for a game, but he discovers he has to play against the dog of the house instead of the master himself.[33]

Although the final metaphor is masculine, this passage could apply to any argument between a radical thinker and 'liberals' in any culture who settle for the *status quo*. Only the ironic use of the word 'nigger' suggests an African writing about Africans.

In this work, which mixes the genres of prose and poetry, relations between men and women are also satirised. The main character, Sissie, who is on a tour of parts of Europe, is constructed as a highly-educated African woman who sees herself as equal to any intellectual. When she meets Marija, a Bavarian housewife who makes lesbian overtures to her, Sissie uses this encounter to fantasise about black men's encounters with white women: 'In her imagination, she was one of these black boys in one of these involvements with white girls in Europe. Struck by some of the stories she had heard, she shivered, absolutely horrified.'[34] When Marija tells Sissie that, because she intends to have only one child 'she was very happy he was a boy', the narrator comments satirically:

> . . .why wish a curse on your child
> Desiring her to be female
> ?
> Beside, my sister,
> The ranks of the wretched are
> Full,
> Are full.[35]

In this imagined free verse response to Marija's recognition of the privileges of men, the narrator universalises the miserable lot of women, but overlooks how women's problems are compounded by their unwillingness to teach their sons to treat women equally with men. Nevertheless, Aidoo's account of a black woman's encounter with Europe is a successful reversal of the more usual theme of European 'quests' to Africa or the East.

Many novels and stories about different races and cultures pivot on the question of how a woman can express her sexuality acceptably in the social and legal organisation of her own culture *and* remain free. But the problems for women of engaging sexually in and across cultures are not the only ones that might be approached in fiction. Women's problems, especially if they belong to a minority class or culture, are not only sexual, but also economic. The unequal power relations between employer and employee are compounded when the employer is a man and the employee a woman from a minority group. In *The Things That Divide Us* (1985), BarbaraNeely [sic] in 'Sisters' illustrates how women's problems in dealing with male employers are similar whatever the class or race of either party. She contrasts the lives of two employees of the same advertising firm: Jackie, the office cleaner, who borrows money from a man who demands sex in place of payment of interest, and Lorisa, the 'token black' seller of advertising who is so afraid of being sacked that she, against her will, agrees to engage sexually with one of her firm's prestigious male clients. At the conclusion, the narrator implies that women should unite against male predators who abuse their economic power. A few contemporary women writers in collections such as *The Things That Divide Us* show the folly of women from any culture trying to revolve their lives sexually around men, whether as lovers, wives or mistresses. But such innovatory fiction is often in the form of short stories and sketches, and tends to emerge in anthologies published by small feminist presses.

8

Conclusion

Reading and writing give us some power to think or to avoid thinking about our experience of the world. 'Politics' in marriage, at work, or even in government, is about power – how it is exerted or experienced by one person in relation to another, or by one group in relation to another group. So when women read a work of fiction, they are engaged in a political act by which they might gain or lose power, depending on how and what they read. The effect of a work of fiction in increasing or decreasing our power depends on the level of our competence as critical readers. Women, who now live politically under a late decadent patriarchy in which a fortunate minority of women have been co-opted as honorary men, must adopt a reading strategy whereby we examine to what extent each work of fiction supports the structure of unequal power relationships between men and women or to what extent the fiction subverts this unequal structure.

Such a reading strategy certainly should not involve a concomitant political strategy of trying to suppress those books that fail to expose patriarchy for what it is. Such censorship, whether institutionalised or unofficial, apart from its undesirability on philosophical grounds, merely serves to provide some of the 'loony feminist nonsense' of the kind that is sent up in magazines such as *Private Eye*. We should, however, make sure that we become aware of the implicit world-views or hidden curricula that we are imbibing through our reading. No woman should any longer have to fall in with fiction which subtly or not so subtly suggests that we should enjoy curtailing our lives in order to conform to the demand that patriarchies have always made for passive and self-sacrificing women. The most provocative fiction not only makes a truthful representation of our world, but also exposes and subverts what is wrong with it.

Recent fiction which subverts the *status quo* of men's dominance over women is often linked with actual political events in the late 1960s and 1970s. In those decades, in a few countries, women in large numbers, if not yet an outright majority, began to rebel against received notions about how they should allow themselves to be dominated by men in the home and at the workplace. So post-1970 women's fiction inherited a refreshing new possibility: to represent this actual historical change for the better in the way a great many women now see themselves as no longer adjuncts to men, but as human beings in their own right. This new breed of fiction was facilitated by a major cultural change that occurred in the 1970s and 1980s – the successful development, firstly, of new publishing houses such as Virago and The Women's Press which cater mainly for women writers and readers, and secondly, of women's studies lists in the catalogues of the mainstream publishing houses.

Novelists such as Marge Piercy, Lisa Alther and Barbara Wilson use their fiction to construe aspects of the 'women's liberation' movement of the 1970s. They give us heroines who have been completely freed from their old social training which was designed to let men exploit them. Their novels are at times concerned with particular phenomena such as 'consciousness-raising' groups and 'battered women's refuges'. Other novels are concerned with how politically active women shifted away from our two centuries-long espousal of men's radical movements, and started to build a second, but this time permanent, women's emancipation movement which emphasises the needs and rights of all women in the home, at work and in society.

I have demonstrated ways of identifying novels which embody marginal or alternative world-views, and subvert debased aspects of the still dominant patriarchal world-views in our society. Once it is published, any worthwhile novel, which is necessarily always a form of cultural expression, becomes part of that society's set of world-views, however marginal the novel might seem. Some recent novels by women, for example, in dealing with the politicisation of women in the 1970s and the 1980s, represent a world in which women love women without subterfuge or guilt. These novels remain on the margin, partly because they are rarely reviewed in the press and partly because the majority public is as outraged by lesbianism almost as much as it is scared by male homosexuality. But a few of these avant-garde women's novels are nevertheless undermining the received idea that women's sexual relationships with each other should be concealed.

Fiction about black and working-class women, who have been even more discounted domestically, socially and economically than most other women, is also making its way into our general culture. Alice Walker's fiction and essays about black American women have been acclaimed by mainstream literary criticism, but most of this area of writing remains neglected. Nicky Edwards's *Mud*, with its creation of an elderly working-class woman, is revealing about the politicisation of women *vis-à-vis* men as well as about lesbianism. Joan Riley's *The Unbelonging* shows us the problems of immigrant West Indian children who are rejected in Britain and exploited by adults, particularly by men. And Jill Miller's *Happy As A Dead Cat* gives us a working-class marriage in which the heroine, despite being encumbered with five children, gets a bank business loan with a woman friend and ditches her exploitative husband. Indeed, even Mrs Thatcher might find this one an elevating read. Many women novelists still write fiction which concentrates on 'love' affairs in which a woman's only real work is to shine up to a man. But alongside such more or less traditional middle-brow women's novels, other world-views are emerging in an 'alternative' fiction which is gaining many followers, especially since the opening of 'women only' bookshops which feature these titles. Some women now follow and read virtually all the fiction from women's presses such as The Women's Press and Virago.

The large changes which are necessary in order to make all women free and equal will only occur if we become aware that, in the perversely powerful field of audio-visual entertainment and advertising, we are being subtly coded to perceive ourselves in a way which mainly serves the profit and well-being of those who have social, sexual and economic power. Although Channel 4, for example, might present programmes which decode such advertising, these programme are rare in comparison with the stereotyped world-views they transmit on many of their other programmes and which the new oligarchies in satellite television will transmit in vulgar variations on almost everything they beam out.

In advertising, for instance, an enlightened Channel 4 programme shows, through a viewer's commentary, that washing-machines need not only be serviced by men for payment and used by women in unpaid labour, but could be repaired by women for payment and used by men to do their own and their family's washing. On the other hand, Channel 4 still carries conventional advertising about washing-machines which show women using them without charging for their labour, and men repairing these machines for payment. I am not suggesting that such advertising should be banned or cumpulsorily re-scripted by a progressive group like Channel 4; after all, most family cleaning is still done by women with minimal help from men. I am suggesting that women should begin to read the subtle coercion in such advertising with its blatant reinforcement of what is supposed to be suitable for 'masculine' men and 'feminine' women.

The reading of worthwhile fiction and thoughtful criticism of fiction are political acts by which women can prepare themselves to have an effect on their world. Virginia Woolf describes, in 'How Should One Read a Book?' (1932), how each individual reader affects both the writer and the cultural climate in which she exists:

> . . . if to read a book as it should be read calls for the rarest qualities of imagination, insight, and judgement, you may perhaps conclude that literature is a very complex art and that it is unlikely that we shall be able, even after a lifetime of reading, to make any valuable contribution to its criticism. We must remain readers; we shall not put on the further glory that belongs to those rare beings who are also critics. But still we have our responsibilities as readers and even our importance. The standards we raise and the judgements we pass steal into the air and become part of the atmosphere . . .[1]

Although Woolf's notion might seem mystical, she is simply indicating how the influence of an important book can spread. Nowadays this sometimes occurs through seminars and other educational activities, but it always happens by means of the words and actions of enthusiastic readers in their everyday lives.

I hope readers who have stayed the course of my book will have been helped to read fiction differently in future. I hope this can be done with more laughter than tears. They will look for, among other things, what is *not* said about women, or for exploitative assumptions about women. They will differentiate between novels that have implicit world-views and hidden curricula which are unpleasantly   self-contradictory   or   attractively   subversive. Moreover, they will seek out novels which imply the rightness of an ideal world in which all women are free, with equal rights, in all fields, with men. And they will pass their judgements accordingly – in speech or in writing or in their actions – thus kicking against the pricks of their everyday existence.

Notes and References

Introduction

1. For a discussion of 'patriarchy', see Kate Millett, *Sexual Politics* (London: Rupert Hart-Davis, 1971); reprinted Virago, 1977, pp. 24–5.
2. Virginia Woolf, *Women and Writing*, introd. Michèle Barrett (London: The Women's Press, 1979) p. 49.
3. Ibid., pp. 49–50.
4. Elaine Showalter, *A Literature of Their Own: British Women Novelists from Brontë to Lessing* (London: Princeton University Press, 1977); reprinted Virago, 1987, pp. 298–319.
5. Patricia Stubbs, *Women and Fiction: Feminism and the Novel 1880–1920* (Brighton: Harvester, 1979; London: Methuen, 1981).
6. See, for example, Hélène Cixous and Catherine Clément, *The Newly Born Woman* (Paris, 1975); trans. Betsy Wing (Manchester: Manchester University Press, 1986) pp. 63–97.
7. See, for example, Pierre Macherey, *A Theory of Literary Production* (Paris, 1966); trans. Geoffrey Wall, London, Routledge, 1978, pp. 79, 85, and 128.

Chapter 1 The 'feminine' and fiction

1. Anthony Burgess, *The Novel Now: A Student's Guide to Contemporary Fiction*, (London: Faber, 1967; new edn, 1971), p. 132.
2. Sigmund Freud, *Introductory Lectures on Psychoanalysis*, 1916–17, trans. James Strachey (London: Hogarth, 1963); reprinted Harmondsworth: Penguin, 1973, Lectures 1–5, pp. 39–128.
3. Cixous and Clément, *The Newly Born Woman*, p. 97.
4. William Wordsworth, *Poetical Works*, ed. Thomas Hutchinson, new edn, rev. Ernest de Selincourt (Oxford University Press, 1936); reprinted 1966, p. 461.
5. 'To George and Tom Keats', December 1817, *Letters of John Keats*, ed. Robert Gittings (Oxford University Press, 1970); reprinted 1982, p. 43.
6. Cixous and Clément, *The Newly Born Woman*, p. 86.
7. Cixous and Clément, *The Newly Born Woman*, pp. 66 and 84.
8. Virginia Woolf, *Women and Writing*, pp. 61–2.

9. Frankie Finn, *Out on the Plain* (London: The Women's Press, 1984) p. 13.

10. Patrick White, *Flaws in the Glass: A Self-Portrait* (London: Jonathan Cape, 1981) p. 155.

11. Dorothy Richardson, *Pointed Roofs* (1915), in *Pilgrimage*, vol. ɪ (London: J. M. Dent, 1938); reissued 1967, p. 29.

12. Virginia Woolf, 'Dorothy Richardson',*Women and Writing*, p. 191.

13. Dorothy Richardson, *Pointed Roofs*, p. 73.

14. Katherine Mansfield, *The Aloe*, first. pub. as *Prelude* (London: Hogarth, 1918); new edn., Virago, 1985, pp. 69–70.

15. Ibid., p. 46.

16. Ibid., pp. 28–9.

17. Ibid., p. 63.

18. Ibid., p. 24.

19. Ibid., p. 28.

20. Ibid., p. 39.

21. Ibid., p. 68.

22. Ibid., p. 69.

23. Elizabeth Wright, *Psychoanalytic Criticism: Theory in Practice* (London: Methuen, 1984) pp. 111–12.

24. Virginia Woolf, *To the Lighthouse*, pp. 142–3.

25. Ibid., p. 144.

26. Ibid., p. 202.

27. Ibid., p. 80.

28. Ibid., pp. 310–20.

29. Ibid., p. 142.

30. Dorothy Richardson, *Pointed Roofs*, pp. 458–60.

31. Ibid., pp. 472–3.

Chapter 2   Sexuality and marriage

1. Kate Millett, *Sexual Politics*, Virago, 1977, pp. 237–335.

2. Rosamond Lehmann, *The Weather in the Streets* (London: Wm. Collins, 1936); reprinted Virago, 1981, p. 383.

3. Elizabeth Bowen, *The House in Paris* (London: Gollancz, 1935); reprinted Harmondsworth: Penguin, 1946, reissued 1983, p. 69.

4. Elaine Showalter, *A Literature of Their Own*, p. 307.

5. Margaret Drabble, *The Middle Ground* (London: Weidenfeld & Nicolson, 1980); reprinted Harmondsworth: Penguin, 1981, pp. 269–70.

6. Kate Chopin, *The Awakening* (USA: Herbert S. Stone & Co., 1899); London: The Women's Press, 1978, p. 7.

7. Ibid., p. 14.

8. Ibid., p. 32.

9. Ibid., p. 33.

10. Ibid., p. 33.

11. Ibid., p. 95.

12. Ibid., pp. 188–9.

13. Miles Franklin, *My Brilliant Career* (Edinburgh: Blackwoods, 1901); reprinted London, Virago, 1980, pp. 222–3.

14. Christina Stead, *The Beauties and the Furies* (London: Peter Davies, 1936); reprinted Virago, 1982, pp. 131–2.

15. Ibid., Virago, pp. 130–1.

16. Christina Stead, *For Love Alone* (London: Peter Davies, 1945); reprinted Virago, 1978, p. 464.

17. Ibid., Virago, p. 500.

18. Christina Stead, *Letty Fox: Her Luck* (London: Peter Davies, 1947); reprinted Virago, 1978, p. 492.

19. Ibid., p. 474.

20. Ibid., p. 5.

21. Ibid., p. 502.

22. Jean Rhys, *After Leaving Mr Mackenzie* (London: Jonathan Cape, 1930); reprinted Harmondsworth: Penguin, 1971, p. 17.

23. Margaret Atwood, *Life Before Man* (Toronto: McClelland & Stewart Ltd, 1979); reprinted London: Virago, 1982, p. 308.

24. Ibid., Virago, p. 316.

25. Fay Weldon, *The Heart of the Country* (London: Hutchinson, 1987; Arrow, 1987) p. 198.

26. Grace Bartram, *Peeling* (London: The Women's Press, 1986) p. 48.

27. Ibid., p. 106.

28. Ibid., p. 78.

29. Lisa Alther, *Original Sins* (New York: Alfred A. Knopf; London, The Women's Press, 1981) p. 470–1.

30. Ibid., pp. 459–60.

31. Ibid., pp. 460–1.

32. Ibid., p. 449.

Chapter 3   Work and 'brilliant' careers

1. Virginia Woolf, 'Women and Fiction', *Women and Writing*, p. 46.

2. 'To Benjamin Bailey', 22 November 1817, *Letters of John Keats*, ed. Robert Gittings, p. 38.

3. Dorothy Richardson, *Pointed Roofs*, p. 390.

4. Gail Braybon and Penny Summerfield, *Out of the Cage: Women's Experiences in Two World Wars* (London: Pandora, 1987, pp. 17–18).

5. Virginia Woolf, *Mrs Dalloway* (London: Hogarth, 1925); reprinted Grafton, 1976, pp. 115–18.

6. Ibid., Grafton, pp. 116–21.

7. Ibid., p. 11.

8. Braybon and Summerfield, p. 138.

9. Winifred Holtby, *South Riding: An English Landscape* (London: Collins, 1936); reprinted Virago, 1988, p. 60.

10. Ibid., Virago, p. 448.

11. Tillie Olsen, *Silences* (London: Virago) pp. 29–30.

12. Buchi Emecheta, *Head Above Water* (London: Fontana, 1986) pp. 242–3.

13. Tillie Olsen, *Silences*, p. 30.

14. Miles Franklin, *My Brilliant Career*, pp. 31–3.

15. Ibid., p. 224.

16. Miles Franklin, *My Career Goes Bung*, pp. 224–5.

17. Ibid., p. 232.

18. Willa Cather, *Lucy Gayheart* (Boston, Mass.: Houghton Mifflin & Co., 1915), revised 1937; London: Virago, 1982, p. 109.

19. Ibid., Virago, p. 134.

20. Ibid., p. 184.

21. Ibid., p. 230.

22. Christina Stead, *Miss Herbert (The Suburban Wife)* (New York: Random House, 1976); reprinted London: Virago, 1979, p. 211.

23. Ibid., Virago, p. 227.

24. Ibid., p. 229.

25. Gaskell, Elizabeth, *Four Short Stories*, introd. Anna Walters (London: Pandora, Routledge, 1983).

26. Storm Jameson, 'A Day Off', *Women Against Men* (Leipzig: Bernhard Tauchnitz, 1933); reprinted London: Virago, 1982, p. 225.

27. Ibid., Virago, pp. 226–7.

28. Ibid., pp. 291–2.

29. Braybon and Summerfield, p. 2.

30. Ibid, p. 124.

31. Ibid, p. 287.

32. Stevie Davies, *Boy Blue* (London: The Women's Press, 1987) pp. 157–8.

33. Ibid., p. 165.

34. Nell Dunn, *Up the Junction* (London: MacGibbon & Kee, 1963); reprinted Virago, 1988, p. 27.

35. Kylie Tennant, *Tiburon* (Sydney: *Bulletin*, 1935); Angus & Robertson, 1972, p. 199.

36. Ibid., Angus & Robertson, p. 337.

37. Kylie Tennant, *The Honey Flow* (Sydney: Angus & Robertson, 1956); paperback, 1983, p. 224.

38. Ibid., paperback, p. 348.

39. Katherine Susannah Prichard, *The Roaring Nineties* (London: Jonathan Cape, 1946); reprinted Virago, 1983, p. 59.

40. Ibid., p. 311.

41. Harry Heseltine, 'Australian Fiction Since 1920', in Geoffrey Dutton (ed.) *The Literature of Australia* (Harmondsworth: Penguin, 1964); revised 1976, pp. 209–210.

42. Katherine Susannah Prichard, *Haxby's Circus* (London: Jonathan Cape, 1930); reprinted Sydney, Angus & Robertson, 1973; paperback, 1979, p. 350.

Chapter 4 Mothers and children

1. D. H. Lawrence, *Sons and Lovers* (London: Methuen, 1913; Harmondsworth: Penguin, 1948); reprinted 1973, p. 44.
2. D. H. Lawrence, *The Rainbow* (London: Methuen, 1915; Harmondsworth: Penguin, 1949); reprinted 1973, pp. 80–1.
3. Doris Lessing, *A Proper Marriage* (London, MacGibbon & Kee, 1965); reprinted Panther, 1975, p. 164.
4. Elizabeth Baines, *The Birth Machine* (London: The Women's Press, 1983) p. 72.
5. Ibid., pp. 94–5.
6. Ibid., pp. 118–19.
7. Dorothy Dinnerstein, *The Mermaid and the Minotaur: Sexual Arrangements and Human Malaise* (New York: Harper & Row, 1976) pp. 76–78.
8. Ibid., p. 81.
9. Edith Wharton, *The Mother's Recompense* (New York: D. Appleton & Co., 1925); reprinted London: Virago, 1986, p. 16.
10. Storm Jameson, *Company Parade, Mirror in Darkness*, vol. ɪ (London: Cassell & Co., 1934); reprinted Virago, 1982, p. 9.
11. Ibid., Virago, p. 18.
12. Storm Jameson, *Journey from the North*, vol. ɪ (London: Collins, 1969); reprinted Virago, 1984, p. 135.
13. Ibid., Virago, p. 88.
14. Storm Jameson, *Company Parade*, pp. 80–1.
15. Joan Barfoot, *Gaining Ground* (Toronto: McGraw-Hill, 1978); reprinted London: The Women's Press, 1980, pp. 139–40.
16. Ibid., The Women's Press, pp. 156–7.
17. Joyce Reiser Kornblatt, *Nothing to Do with Love* (New York: Viking Press, 1981); reprinted London: The Women's Press, 1982, p. 95.
18. Joyce Cary, 'A Hot Day', *Spring Song and Other Stories* (London: Michael Joseph, 1960) pp. 113–4.
19. Ibid., p. 114.
20. Joyce Cary, 'Babes in the Wood', *Spring Song and Other Stories*, p. 43.
21. Ibid., pp. 43–4.
22. Christina Stead, *The Man Who Loved Children* (New York: Simon and Schuster, 1940; London: Peter Davies, 1941); reprinted Harmondsworth: Penguin, 1970, pp. 519–21.
23. Ivy Compton-Burnett, *The Present and the Past* (London: Victor Gollancz 1953); reprinted Harmondsworth: Penguin, 1972, pp. 162–3.
24. Virginia Woolf, *To the Lighthouse*, pp. 12–13.
25. Ibid., p. 107.
26. Ibid., pp. 93–4.
27. May Sinclair, *Life and Death of Harriett Frean* (London: Wm. Collins, 1922); reprinted Virago, 1980, pp. 1–3.
28. Ibid., Virago, pp. 7–8.
29. Ibid., pp. 24–5.

30. Judith Barrington, in Stephanie Dowrick and Sybil Grundberg (eds) *Why Children?* (London: The Women's Press) p. 154.

Chapter 5   Alternatives to marriage

1. May Sarton, *The Magnificent Spinster* (New York: W. W. Norton, 1985); reprinted London: The Women's Press, 1986, p. 58.
2. Ibid., The Women's Press, p. 103.
3. Joanna Russ, *On Strike Against God* (USA: Out & Out Books, 1980); reprinted London: The Women's Press, 1987, pp. 6–7.
4. Ibid., The Women's Press, pp. 54–6.
5. Marge Piercy, *The High Cost of Living* (USA: Doubleday & Co., 1978); reprinted London, The Women's Press, 1979, pp. 2–3.
6. Ibid., The Women's Press, p. 184.
7. Ibid., pp. 196–7.
8. Cixous and Clément, *The Newly Born Woman*, p. 136.
9. Marge Piercy, *The High Cost of Living*, p. 19.
10. Grace Bartram, *Peeling*, pp. 106–7.
11. Ibid., p. 132.
12. Elizabeth Jolley, *Miss Peabody's Inheritance* (Queensland: University of Queensland Press, 1983) pp. 139–41.
13. Ibid., p.58.
14. May Sarton, *A Reckoning* (New York: W. W. Norton, 1978; London: Victor Gollancz, 1980); reprinted The Women's Press, 1984, p. 13.
15. Ibid., p. 243.
16. Virginia Woolf, *Mrs Dalloway*, pp. 30–3.
17. Ibid., p. 43.
18. May Sarton, *A Reckoning*, p. 252.
19. Nicky Edwards, *Mud* (London: The Women's Press, 1986) p. 76.
20. Alice Walker, *The Color Purple* (New York: Harcourt Brace Jovanovich, 1983; London: The Women's Press, 1983) pp. 97–8.
21. Nicky Edwards, *Mud*, pp. 70 and 85.

Chapter 6   Politics and war

1. Kate Millett, *Sexual Politics*, p. 21.
2. Ibid., p. 25.
3. Ibid., p.22.
4. Storm Jameson, *None Turn Back, Mirror in Darkness*, vol. III (London: Cassell & Co., 1936); reprinted Virago, 1984, p. 256.
5. Jean Devanny, *Cindie* (London: Robert Hale, 1949); reprinted Virago, 1986, p. 311.
6. Ibid., Virago, p. 173.
7. Christina Stead, *Seven Poor Men of Sydney* (London: Peter Davies, 1934) reprinted Australia: Angus & Robertson, 1965, paperback 1981, pp. 205.

8. Ibid., paperback, p. 205.
9. Christina Stead, *Cotters' England* (London: Secker & Warburg, 1967); reprinted Virago, 1980, pp. 276–90.
10. Ibid., Virago, p. 291.
11. Ibid., pp. 296–7.
12. Meridel Le Sueur, *The Girl* (USA: West End Press, 1978); reprinted London: The Women's Press, 1982, pp. 99–100.
13. Ibid., The Women's Press, p. 75
14. Ibid., p. 146.
15. Barbara Wilson, *Ambitious Women* (USA: Spinsters Ink Ltd., 1982); reprinted London: The Women's Press, 1983, pp. 214–5.
16. Ibid., The Women's Press, pp. 47–8.
17. Ibid., p. 154.
18. Nicky Edwards, *Mud*, p. 30.
19. Ibid., p. 168.
20. Ibid., p.73.
21. Rebecca West, *The Return of the Soldier* (London: Nisbet, 1918); reprinted Virago, 1980, pp. 13–14.
22. Ibid., Virago, p. 147.
23. Ibid., p. 184.
24. Ibid., p. 187.
25. Ibid., pp. 153–4.
26. Ibid., pp. 25–9.
27. Ibid., p. 181.

Chapter 7 Beyond racial stereotypes

1. Naipaul, V. S., *The Mimic Men* (London, André Deutsch, 1967); reprinted Harmondsworth: Penguin, 1969, pp. 46–7.
2. Jhabvala, Ruth Prawer, *Three Continents* (London: John Murray, 1987); reprinted Harmondsworth: Penguin, 1988, p. 162.
3. Ruth Prawer Jhabvala, 'In the Mountain', *How I Became a Holy Mother* (London: John Murray, 1976) p. 31.
4. Ruth Prawer Jhabvala, 'Desecration', *How I Became a Holy Mother*, p. 189.
5. Ibid., p. 203.
6. Padma Perera,'Pilgrimage', *Birthday Deathday* (London: The Women's Press, 1985) p. 88.
7. Padma Perera, 'Weather Report', *Birthday Deathday*, pp. 147–67.
8. Jean Rhys, 'Let Them Call It Jazz', *Tigers Are Better-Looking* (London: André Deutsch, 1968); reprinted Harmondsworth: Penguin, 1972, pp. 60–1.
9. Ibid., Penguin, p. 63.
10. Maureen Duffy, *Wounds* (London: Hutchinson, 1969); reprinted London: Methuen, 1984, p. 56.
11. Joan Riley, *Waiting in the Twilight* (London: The Women's Press, 1987) p. 16.

12. Ibid., pp. 21–2.

13. Ibid., pp. 164–5.

14. Joan Riley, *The Unbelonging* (London: The Women's Press, 1985).

15. Alice Walker, *The Third Life of Grange Copeland* (New York: Harcourt Brace Jovanovich, 1970); reprinted London; The Women's Press, 1985, p. 20.

16. Ibid., The Women's Press, p. 21.

17. Ibid., p. 47.

18. Ibid., pp. 55–7.

19. Ibid., p. 55.

20. Julia Kristeva, 'Woman Can Never Be Defined', in Elaine Marks and Isabelle de Courtivron (eds), *New French Feminisms* (Brighton: The Harvester Press, 1981); reprinted 1986, p. 141.

21. Alice Walker, *Meridian* (New York: Harcourt Brace Jovanovich, 1976); reprinted London: The Women's Press, 1982, pp. 7–8.

22. Simone de Beauvoir, 'From an Interview', *New French Feminisms*, p. 148.

23. Alice Walker, *Meridian*, pp. 40–1.

24. Ibid., p. 58.

25. Ibid., pp. 87–8.

26. Ibid., pp. 227–8.

27. Nadine Gordimer, *Burger's Daughter* (London: Jonathan Cape, 1979) p. 302.

28. Ibid., p. 199.

29. Ibid., p. 159.

30. Ibid., pp. 134–5.

31. Olive Schreiner, *From Man to Man* (London: T. Fisher Unwin, 1926); reprinted Virago, 1982, p. 305.

32. Ibid., Virago, p. 439.

33. Ama Ata Aidoo, *Our Sister Killjoy: Or Reflections from a Black-Eyed Squint* (London: Longman, 1977) p. 6.

34. Ibid., p. 61.

35. Ibid., p. 51.

Chapter 8   Conclusion

1. Virginia Woolf, 'How Should One Read a Book?', *The Common Reader*, vol. 2 (London: Hogarth, 1932); reprinted Hogarth (Chatto & Windus) 1986, p. 269.

Bibliography

Fiction: 101 suggestions for lively reading

Aidoo, Ama Ata, *No Sweetness Here* (London: Longman, 1970; reprinted 1979). [Short stories.]

——*Our Sister Killjoy: Or Reflections from a Black-Eyed Squint* (London: Longman, 1977).

Alther, Lisa, *Original Sins* (New York: Alfred A. Knopf; London: The Women's Press, 1981).

Atwood, Margaret, *The Edible Woman* (Toronto: McClelland & Stewart (London: Pandora, Routledge, 1983).

——*Life Before Man* (Toronto: McClelland & Stewart Ltd, 1979; reprinted London: Virago, 1982).

Baines, Elizabeth, *The Birth Machine* (London: The Women's Press, 1983.)

Bambara, Toni Cade, *The Sea Birds Are Still Alive* (New York: Random House, 1982; London: The Women's Press, 1984). [Short stories.]

Barfoot, Joan, *Gaining Ground* (Toronto: McGraw-Hill, 1978; London: The Women's Press, 1980).

Barnard Eldershaw, Marjorie [pseudonym of Marjorie Barnard and Flora Eldershaw], *Tomorrow and Tomorrow and Tomorrow* (Melbourne: Georgian House [censored] 1947; London: Virago [uncensored], 1983).

Bartram, Grace, *Peeling* (London: The Women's Press, 1986).

Bowen, Elizabeth, *The House in Paris* (London: Gollancz, 1935; reprinted Harmondsworth: Penguin, 1946; reissued 1976).

Cather, Willa, *The Song of the Lark* (Boston, Mass.: Houghton Mifflin & Co., 1915, revised 1937; London: Virago, 1982).

——*Lucy Gayheart* (New York: Alfred Knopf Inc., 1935; London: Virago, 1985).

Chopin, Kate, *The Awakening* (USA: Herbert S. Stone & Co., 1899; London: The Women's Press, 1978).

Compton-Burnett, Ivy, *The Present and the Past* (London: Victor Gollancz, 1953; reprinted Harmondsworth: Penguin, 1972).

Conlon, Faith, *et al.* (eds), *The Things That Divide Us* (Washington: The Seal Press, 1985; London: Sheba Feminist Publishers, 1986). [Short stories]

Cooper, Lettice, *Fenny* (London: Victor Gollancz, 1953; reprinted London: Virago, 1987).

Davies, Stevie, *Boy Blue* (London: The Women's Press, 1987).

Devanny, Jean, *Cindie* (London: Robert Hale, 1949; reprinted London: Virago, 1986).

H. D. [Doolittle, Hilda], *Bid Me to Live* (New York: Grove Press Inc., 1960; London: Virago, 1984).

Duffy, Maureen, *Wounds* (London: Hutchinson, 1969; reprinted London: Methuen, 1984).

Dunn, Nell, *Up the Junction* (London: MacGibbon & Kee, 1963; reprinted London: Virago, 1988.

——*Poor Cow* (London: MacGibbon & Kee, 1967; reprinted London: Virago, 1988).

Edwards, Nicky, *Mud* (London: The Women's Press, 1986).

Fairbairns, Zoe, *Closing* (London: Methuen, 1987; reprinted 1988).

Finn, Frankie, *Out on the Plain* (London: The Women's Press, 1984).

Franklin, Miles, *My Brilliant Career* (Edinburgh: Blackwoods, 1901; Australia: Angus & Robertson, 1965, 3rd edn, 1974; London: Virago, 1980).

——*My Career Goes Bung* (Melbourne: Georgian House, 1946; London: ˜ Virago, 1981).

Gordimer, Nadine, *The Lying Days* (London: Victor Gollancz, 1953; reprinted London: Virago, 1983.

——*Occasion for Loving* (London: Victor Gollancz, 1963; reprinted London: Virago, 1983).

——*Burger's Daughter* (London: Jonathan Cape, 1979).

Harrower, Elizabeth, *The Long Prospect* (London: Cassell & Co., 1958; Australia: Sun Books, 1966; Angus & Robertson, 1979).

Holtby, Winifred, *Anderby Wold* (London: John Lane at the Bodley Head, 1923; reprinted London: Virago, 1981).

——*South Riding: An English Landscape* (London: Collins, 1936; reprinted London: Virago, 1988).

Jameson, Storm, *Women Against Men* (Leipzig: Bernhard Tauchnitz, 1933; London: Virago, 1982).

——*Company Parade*, vol. I *Mirror in Darkness* (London: Cassell & Co., 1934; reprinted London: Virago, 1982).

——*Love in Winter*, vol. II, *Mirror in Darkness* (London: Cassell & Co., 1935; reprinted London: Virago, 1984).

——*None Turn Back*, vol. III, *Mirror in Darkness* (London: Cassell & Co., 1936; reprinted London: Virago, 1984).

Jenkins, Elizabeth, *The Tortoise and the Hare* (London: Victor Gollancz, 1945; reprinted London: Virago, 1983).

Jhabvala, Ruth Prawer, *Heat and Dust* (London: John Murray, 1975).

——*How I Became a Holy Mother* (London: John Murray, 1976). [Short stories.]

——*Three Continents* (London: John Murray, 1987; reprinted Harmondsworth: Penguin, 1988).

Jolley, Elizabeth, *Mr. Scobie's Riddle* (Australia: Penguin, 1983).

——*Miss Peabody's Inheritance* (Queensland: University of Queensland Press, 1983).

Kornblatt, Joyce Reiser, *Nothing to Do with Love* (New York: Viking Press, 1981; London: The Women's Press, 1982).
Laurence, Margaret, *A Jest of God* (Toronto: McClelland & Stewart, 1966; London: Macmillan, 1966; reprinted London: Virago, 1987).
Lehmann, Rosamond, *A Note in Music* (London: Chatto & Windus, 1930; reprinted London: Virago, 1982).
Lessing, Doris, *The Grass Is Singing* (London: Michael Joseph, 1950; reprinted Harmondsworth: Penguin, 1961, 1976).
——*Martha Quest*, Book 1, *Children of Violence* (London, MacGibbon & Kee, 1965; Panther, 1966, reprinted 1975).
——*A Proper Marriage*, Book 2, *Children of Violence* (London: MacGibbon & Kee, 1965; Panther, 1966, reprinted 1975).
Le Sueur, Meridel, *The Girl* (USA: West End Press, 1978; London: The Women's Press, 1982).
McLeod, Marion and Lydia, Wevers, *One Whale, Singing and Other Stories from New Zealand* (Auckland, OUP, 1985; The Women's Press, 1986). [Short stories.]
Mansfield, Katherine, *The Aloe*, first published as *Prelude* (London: Hogarth, 1918; New Zealand: Port Nicholson Press, 1982; Manchester: Carcanet, 1983; London: Virago, new edn, 1985).
Mayor, F. M., *The Rector's Daughter* (London: Hogarth, 1924; reprinted London: Virago, 1987).
Miller, Betty, *On the Side of the Angels* (London: Robert Hale, 1945; reprinted London: Virago, 1985).
Miller, Jill, *Happy As a Dead Cat* (London: The Women's Press, 1983).
Munro, Alice, *Lives of Girls and Women* (New York: McGraw-Hill, 1971; London: Allen Lane, 1973; reprinted Harmondsworth: Penguin, 1982).
——*The Beggar Maid* (Toronto: Macmillan, 1978; Harmondsworth: Allen Lane and Penguin, 1980).
Perera, Padma, *Birthday Deathday* (London: The Women's Press, 1985). [Short stories.]
Piercy, Marge, *The High Cost of Living* (USA: Doubleday & Co., 1978; London: The Women's Press, 1979).
Plath Sylvia, *The Bell Jar* (London: Heinemann, 1963; reprinted London: Faber & Faber, 1966).
Prichard, Katherine Susannah, *Haxby's Circus* (London: Jonathan Cape, 1930; reprinted Sydney: Angus & Robertson, 1973; paperback, 1979).
——*The Roaring Nineties* (London: Jonathan Cape, 1946; reprinted London: Virago, 1983).
Pym, Barbara, *Crampton Hodnet* (London: Macmillan, 1985).
——*An Academic Question* (London: Macmillan, 1986).
Rhys, Jean, *After Leaving Mr Mackenzie* (London: Jonathan Cape, 1930; London: André Deutsch, 1969; Harmondsworth: Penguin, 1971).
——*Good Morning, Midnight* (London: Constable, 1939; London: André Deutsch, 1967; Harmondsworth: Penguin, 1969).
——*Tigers Are Better-Looking* (London: André Deutsch, 1968; Harmondsworth: Penguin, 1972).
Richardson, Dorothy, *Pointed Roofs* (1915), *Backwater* (1916), *Hon-*

eycomb (1917), *Pilgrimage*, vol. I (London: J. M. Dent, 1938, reissued 1967; reprinted London: Virago, 1979).

Richardson, Henry Handel, *The Getting of Wisdom* (London: Wm. Heinemann, 1910; reprinted London: Virago, 1981).

Riley, Elizabeth, *All That False Instruction* (London: Angus & Robertson, 1975; paperback, 1981).

Riley, Joan, *The Unbelonging* (London: The Women's Press, 1985).

——*Waiting in the Twilight* (London: The Women's Press, 1987).

Roberts Michèle, *The Book of Mrs Noah* (London: Methuen, 1987).

Russ, Joanna, *On Strike Against God* (USA: Out & Out Books, 1980; London: The Women's Press, 1987).

Sarton, May, *As We Are Now* (New York: W. W. Norton, 1973; London: Victor Gollancz, 1974; reprinted London: The Women's Press, 1983).

——*A Reckoning* (London: Victor Gollancz, 1980; reprinted London: The Women's Press, 1984).

——*The Magnificent Spinster* (New York: W. W. Norton, 1985; London: The Women's Press, 1986).

Schreiner, Olive, *From Man to Man* (London: T. Fisher Unwin; 1926 reprinted London: Virago, 1982).

Sinclair, May, *The Three Sisters* (London: Macmillan, 1914; reprinted London Virago, 1982).

——*Mary Olivier: A Life* (London: Macmillan, 1919; reprinted London: Virago, 1980.

——*Life and Death of Harriet Frean* (London: Wm. Collins, 1922; reprinted London: Virago, 1980).

Stead, Christina, *Seven Poor Men of Sydney* (London: Peter Davies, 1934; Australia: Angus & Robertson, 1965, paperback, 1981).

——*The Beauties and the Furies* (London: Peter Davies, 1936; reprinted London: Virago, 1982).

——*The Man Who Loved Children* (New York: Simon & Schuster, 1940; London: Peter Davies, 1941; reprinted Harmondsworth: Penguin, 1970).

——*For Love Alone* (London: Peter Davies, 1945; reprinted London: Virago, 1978).

——*Letty Fox: Her Luck* (London: Peter Davies, 1947; reprinted London: Virago, 1978).

——*Cotters' England*, original title *Dark Place of the Heart* (New York: Holt, Rinehart & Winston, 1966); as *Cotter's England* (London: Secker & Warburg, 1967; reprinted London: Virago, 1980).

——*Miss Herbert (The Suburban Wife)* (New York: Random House, 1976; London: Virago, 1979).

Tennant, Kylie, *Tiburon* (Sydney: *Bulletin*, 1935; Angus & Robertson, 1972).

——*The Honey Flow* (Australia: Angus & Robertson, 1956; paperback, 1983).

Walker, Alice, *The Third Life of Grange Copeland* (New York: Harcourt Brace Jovanovich, 1970; London: The Women's Press, 1985).

——*Meridian* (New York: Harcourt Brace Jovanovich, 1976; reprinted London: The Women's Press, 1982).

——*The Color Purple* (New York: Harcourt Brace Jovanovich, 1983; London: The Women's Press, 1983).
West, Rebecca, *The Return of the Soldier* (London: Nisbet, 1918; reprinted London: Virago, 1980).
Wharton, Edith, *The House of Mirth* (New York: D. Appleton & Co., 1905; London: Constable, 1966; reprinted Harmondsworth: Penguin, 1979).
——*The Mother's Recompense* (New York: D. Appleton & Co., 1925; London: Virago, 1986).
Wilson, Barbara, *Ambitious Women* (USA: Spinsters Ink Ltd., 1982; London: The Women's Press, 1983).
Woolf, Virginia, *Mrs Dalloway* (London: Hogarth, 1925; Grafton, 1976, reprinted 1987).
——*To The Lighthouse* (London: Hogarth, 1927; reprinted 1967).
Young, E. H., *Chatterton Square* (London: Jonathan Cape, 1947; reprinted London: Virago, 1987).

Scholarly and not so scholarly works: social and literary criticism, autobiography, letters

Arcana, Judith, *Every Mother's Son: The Role of Mothers in the Making of Men* (London: The Women's Press, 1983).
Batsleer, J., *et al.*, *Rewriting English: Cultural Politics of Gender and Class* (London: Methuen, 1985).
Beauvoir, Simone de, *The Second Sex* (Paris: 1949; trans. H. M. Parshley, London: Jonathan Cape, 1953; Harmondsworth, Penguin, 1972; reprinted 1986).
Braybon, Gail and Penny Summerfield, *Out of the Cage: Women's Experiences in Two World Wars* (London: Pandora, Routledge & Kegan Paul, 1987).
Cartledge, Sue and Joanna Ryan, *Sex and Love: New Thoughts on Old Contradictions* (London: The Women's Press, 1983).
Cixous, Hélène and Clément, Catherine, *La Jeune Née* (Paris: Union Générale d'Editions, 1975); *The Newly Born Woman*, trans. Betsy Wing, (Manchester: Manchester University Press, 1986).
Culler, Jonathan, *On Deconstruction: Theory and Criticism after Structuralism* (London: Routledge & Kegan Paul, 1983).
Daly, Mary, *Gyn/Ecology: The Metaethics of Radical Feminism* (Boston: Beacon Press, 1978; London: The Women's Press, 1979).
——*Pure Lust: Elemental Feminist Philosophy* (London: The Women's Press, 1984).
Davis, Angela, *Women, Race & Class* (New York: Random House, 1981; London: The Women's Press, 1982).
Davis, Lennard J., *Resisting Novels: Ideology and Fiction* (London and New York: Methuen, 1987).
Dinnerstein, Dorothy, *The Mermaid and the Minotaur: Sexual Arrangements and Human Malaise* (New York: Harper & Row, 1976).
Dowrick, Stephanie and Sybil Grundberg (eds), *Why Children?* (London: The Women's Press, 1980).

Duchen, Claire, *Feminism in France: From May '68 to Mitterrand* (London: Routledge & Kegan Paul, 1986).

Dworkin, Andrea, *Pornography: Men Possessing Women* (London: The Women's Press, 1981).

Eagleton, Terry, *Criticism and Ideology* (London: Verso, 1978).

Emecheta, Buchi, *Head Above Water: An Autobiography* (London: Fontana, 1986).

Ernst, Sheila and Marie Maguire (eds), *Living with the Sphinx: Papers from the Women's Therapy Centre* (London: The Women's Press, 1987).

Greene, Gail and Coppelia Khan (eds), *Making a Difference: Feminist Literary Criticism* (London: Methuen, 1983).

Grewal, Shabnam, *et al.*, *Charting the Journey: Writings by Black and Third World Women* (London: Sheba Feminist Publishers, 1988).

Griffin, Susan, *Women and Nature: The Roaring Inside Her* (New York: Harper & Row, 1978; London: The Women's Press, 1984).

——*Pornography and Silence: Culture's Revenge Against Nature* (New York: Harper & Row, 1981; London: The Women's Press, 1984).

——*Made from this Earth: Selections from her Writing, 1967–1982* (London: The Women's Press, 1982).

Harford, Barbara and Sarah Hopkins (eds), *Greenham Common: Women at the Wire* (London: The Women's Press, 1984).

Jacobus, Mary (ed.), *Women Writing and Writing about Women* (London: Croom Helm, 1984).

Macherey, Pierre, *Pour une Théorie de la Production Littéraire* (Paris: Librairie François Maspero, 1966; *A Theory of Literary Production*, trans. Geoffrey Wall, London: Routledge & Kegan Paul, 1978).

Marks, Elaine and Isabelle de Courtivron (eds), *New French Feminisms: an Anthology* (Brighton: Harvester Press, 1981; reprinted 1986).

Millett, Kate, *Sexual Politics* (London: Rupert Hart-Davis, 1971; reprinted London: Virago, 1977).

Moers, Ellen, *Literary Women: The Great Writers* (London: The Women's Press, 1978).

Moi, Toril, *Sexual/Textual Politics: Feminist Literary Theory* (London: Methuen, 1985).

——(ed.), *The Kristeva Reader* (Oxford: Basil Blackwell, 1986, reprinted 1987).

Monteith, Moira (ed.), *Women's Writing: A Challenge to Theory* (Brighton: Harvester Press, 1986).

Olsen, Tillie, *Silences* (New York: Delacorte Press, 1979; reprinted London: Virago, 1980).

Pym, Barbara, in Hazel Holt and Hilary Pym (eds), *A Very Private Eye: The Diaries, Letters, and Notebooks* (London: Macmillan, 1984; reprinted Panther Books, 1985).

Radway, Janice, *Reading the Romance: Women, Patriarchy and Popular Literature* (USA; University of North Carolina Press, 1984; London: Verso, 1987).

Rhys, Jean, in Francis Wyndham and Diana Melly (eds), *Letters 1931–1966* (London: André Deutsch, 1984; reprinted Harmondsworth: Penguin, 1985).

Rimmon-Kenan, Shlomith, *Narrative Fiction: Contemporary Poetics* (London: Methuen, 1983).

Russ, Joanna, *How to Suppress Women's Writing* (Austin: University of Texas Press, 1983; London: The Women's Press, 1983).

Showalter, Elaine, *A Literature of Their Own: British Women Novelists from Brontë to Lessing* (London: Princeton University Press, 1977; reprinted London: Virago, 1978, revised 1982).

——(ed.), *The New Feminist Criticism: Essays on Women, Literature, and Theory* (New York: Pantheon Books, 1985; reprinted London: Virago, 1986).

Stubbs, Patricia, *Women and Fiction: Feminism and the Novel 1880–1920* (Brighton: Harvester Press, 1979; London: Methuen, 1981).

Todorov, Tzvetan, *Introduction to Poetics* (London: Hutchinson, 1964).

Tompkins, Jane P., 'The reader in history: the changing shape of literary response', in J. P. Tompkins (ed.), *Reader-Response Criticism: From Formalism to Post-Structuralism* (Baltimore, Md.: Johns Hopkins Press, 1980, pp. 201–32).

Walker, Alice, *In Search of Our Mothers' Gardens: Womanist Prose* (New York: Harcourt Brace Jovanovich, 1983; reprinted London: The Women's Press, 1984).

Woolf, Virginia, *A Room of One's Own* (London: Hogarth, 1928; reprinted Harmondsworth: Penguin, 1977).

——*The Common Reader* (London: Hogarth, 1932; reprinted Hogarth (Chatto & Windus, 1986).

——*Three Guineas* (London: Hogarth, 1938; reprinted Harmondsworth: Penguin, 1977).

——*Women and Writing*, introd. Michèle Barrett (London: The Women's Press, 1979).

Index